# Collins *gem*

# Flags

W9-CTE-953

Every effort has been made to include information which is as accurate and up-to-date as possible at the time of going to press. However, flag information – in particular for countries whose constitutional status is changing – may be subject to revision.

The publishers would like to thank Michael Faul and the late Dr William Crampton of the Flag Institute for generously providing advice and detailed information on many of the flags contained in this book. We would also like to thank those embassies and consulates who verified flag design and other information.

Original text by Carol P. Shaw

HarperCollins*Publishers*
Westerhill Road
Bishopbriggs
Glasgow G64 2QT

www.collins.co.uk

First published 1986
This edition published 2004

Reprint 10 9 8 7 6 5 4 3 2 1

ISBN 0-00-716526-9

Typeset by Davidson Pre-Press Graphics Ltd, Glasgow

Printed in Italy by Amadeus S.r.l.

# CONTENTS

# INTRODUCTION

### The History of Flags

Flags and flag-like emblems in a variety of ever-changing styles and shapes have been used for over 5,000 years. Originally used for identification in war and at sea, the first flag-like objects, or vexilloids, were solid, such as carvings of animals, birds or abstract shapes, held aloft on poles. To these were attributed the power to grant protection and victory to their bearers. The Romans used vexilloids (as in the eagle standards of the legions) but they were also the first to introduce cloth banners to the West.

Crusaders fighting in the Holy Land in the 12th and 13th centuries used flags, and many now-familiar designs originated there. The Cross was an obvious symbol to unite the Europeans, and heraldic rules developed to regulate the designs (see opposite). Rectangular banners hung from vertical instead of horizontal poles, were preferred as more practical than the previous long, trailing pennants.

Banners in the Middle Ages generally represented royals, families or cities. National flags did not emerge clearly until the 17th century: for example, in 1606 came the first flag of Great Britain after the 1603 union of Scotland and England under James VI and I. Most flags used today evolved from 18th- and 19th-century nationalist and revolutionary movements.

Per Pale

Per Fess

Quarterly

Per Bend

Per Bend Sinister

Per Saltire

Tierced in Pale

Tierced in Fess

Gyronny

Checky

Chief

Base

Pale

Fess

Saltire

Cross

Canton

Border

The influence of heraldic shields can be seen in the designs of many Western flags.

**The Shapes of Flags**

Almost all modern flags are rectangular, but this is a fairly recent convention. In medieval times there were many different flag shapes, ranging from a pennant tied to the top of a knight's lance, to the pennants and streamers fixed to a ship's masthead. Opposite are some typical shapes, all still in use: the Swiss flag is square, while Nepal's is a double pennant design. Triangular burgees are flown on yachts, and swallow-tail flags, usually with a tongue (a third pointed tail between the other two), are used in Scandinavian countries as naval ensigns. More unusual designs, such as the medieval gonfanons and oriflammes, are used in pageants and displays.

**The Symbolism of Flags**

Flags share common meanings, and older designs often influence new flags. The obvious feature in older Christian countries' flags is the Cross: plain, as in the English flag; a saltire, as in the Scots; or off-centred, as in Scandinavia. But the most popular design is the tricolour: first used in the Netherlands, its association with the 1789 French Revolution gave it great significance for radical movements.

Colours are often symbolic. Red is linked with Socialism, courage, danger, blood or revolution. White means peace, faith in God or surrender; orange means

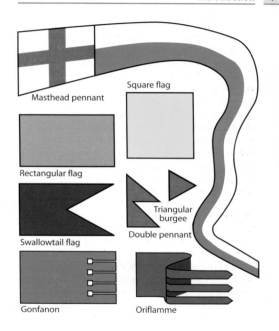

Masthead pennant

Square flag

Rectangular flag

Swallowtail flag

Triangular burgee

Double pennant

Gonfanon

Oriflamme

courage and sacrifice; green means safety, agriculture or Islam; yellow means wealth or mineral riches; and black means mourning, a sad past or strength.

Groups of colours are also used to express ideals. The blue, white and red of the French and American flags were associated with revolution and freedom and were used in the 19th century by areas seeking independence from imperial rule. Red, yellow and green, the Ethiopian colours, were used first by Ghana then by other new African nations in the 1950s and '60s, to express freedom and a desire for African unity; they were known as the Pan-African colours. Similar sentiments were expressed in the Pan-Arab colours of red, white, black and green, used in the flags of many Gulf states as they emerged into independence from Turkish Ottoman domination. The white, blue and red of Russia were used by the Pan-Slav movement in Eastern Europe in the mid-19th century in their fight for freedom from the Hapsburg Empire. Some of these Slav flags reappeared after the break-up of the Communist bloc in Eastern Europe.

Two countries, the Union of Soviet Socialist Republics (USSR) and Yugoslavia, both split apart in the 1990s. As their flags influenced the successor states, they should be explained. The USSR resulted from the Russian Revolution of 1917. At its height, this

Communist state included Russia and 14 other modern countries in Eastern Europe and Central Asia. Internal troubles caused the Union to weaken, and it dissolved in 1991, leaving its members independent. When the Austro-Hungarian Empire disintegrated after World War I, the southern parts of Bosnia-Herzegovina, Croatia and Slovenia joined with Serbia, Montenegro and Macedonia to form Yugoslavia. This country gradually dissolved in the 1990s as first Slovenia and Croatia and then other parts broke away from it.

## Official and Unofficial Flags

There are many unofficial flags. Some have not been officially adopted, but are in general and permitted use. Others are of ethnic, religious or political organisations. Many of these are tolerated, even without official permission. Others are seen by governments as emblems of rebellion and forbidden.

Unofficial flags do not always stay unofficial. When Latvia, Estonia and Lithuania were part of the USSR, they treasured their former flags, even though banned by the government. When the countries regained independence, the old flags returned as the official national flags.

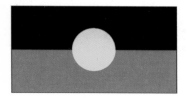

Aboriginal
Peoples' Flag

In Australia a flag was designed for the Aborigine people. It was unofficial at first. Later, the Australian government gave it official recognition as an ethnic flag along with the flag of the Torres Strait Islands.

Others remain unofficial and even banned. The flags of West Papua in Indonesia, Kanaky in French Polynesia and Kurdistan in Turkey and Iraq are separatist emblems and banned by the countries concerned. If the groups using these flags achieve their aims, the flags may then become official.

If an unofficial flag is non-political, there is usually no objection to its use, as long as it does not take the place of an official flag. In Britain, examples of such are some city flags, the flags of commercial companies, religious flags and personal flags. When using any of these, it is advisable to fly the national flag with them and in the place of honour.

Olympic Flag

United Nations Flag

Red Cross

Red Crescent

European Union

## The Uses of Flags

Of course, it is not just nation states which have their own flags. All kinds of organisations, from military and civic to religious, political and industrial, have their own banners. In fact, a flag can be used by any group of people to express a common interest or purpose. Most towns, cities and provinces have their own flags, while heads of state – monarchs and presidents – have their emblems too. The best-known non-national flags are those of international organisations. These include the United Nations flag of blue and white with an olive wreath of peace around a world map, the Olympic flag with five linked rings, the Geneva Convention flags of the Red Cross and Red Crescent, and the European Union flag of twelve gold stars on blue.

Flags have also been used for signalling. Semaphore is a system used on land, although a type of semaphore is also used at sea over short distances. Signal codes, with flags representing numbers, were developed for use at sea during the 18th century, and the International Code has continually been improved since its introduction in 1857. It initially included 70,000 signals and used 18 flags. Each flag signifies a letter of the alphabet and, when flown singly, has a separate meaning of its own. Sailors still have to learn how to hoist and read signals even though modern methods of communication have left them near-obsolete.

## Ensigns

Ensigns are flags used at sea. They may be the same as the land flag or different. The reasons for the differences vary with the country concerned. There may be different naval and civil ensigns. The naval ensign is for warships. The civil ensign is for all privately-owned vessels. All ensigns are national flags, because they show nationality.

The United States has the same flag on land as the naval ensign and civil ensign. The United Kingdom has three ensigns. The naval ensign is the White Ensign, white with a red cross and the Union Flag in the first quarter. The

British White,
Red and Blue
Ensigns

civil ensign is red with the Union Flag. The state ensign
is blue with the Union Flag. This usually has the badge of
a yacht club, dependency or government department.

As a quick guide, Scandinavian naval ensigns are
swallow-tailed, and civil ensigns square-ended. If a
Latin American country has two flags, that with the
badge is the naval ensign, that without it the civil
ensign. A white flag with a national flag and either
a cross or badge is usually a naval ensign. A red flag
with a national flag is usually a civil ensign.

**The Parts of a Flag**

When flags are shown, the flagpole is normally assumed to be on the left of the observer's view. The side then visible is called the *obverse*, the other being the *reverse*. For design and orientation, flags are said to be divided into four quarters, each of which is called a *canton*. The two cantons by the pole are known as the *hoist*, and the other two are called the *fly*. Confusingly, the upper hoist canton (where many of the design features on flags are located) is also called simply the *canton*. (See the illustration below.)

The standard measurements of a flag, given as a proportion of width to length, constitute its *ratio*; ratios are given for flags throughout this book.

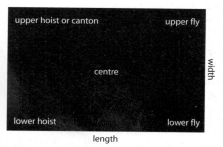

The parts of a flag

# GLOSSARY

***Arms:*** The official heraldic symbols of a nation or family, including a shield with distinctive devices and often supporters (figures on either side of the shield), a crest (a heraldic symbol above the shield) and other insignia. Normally, arms appear on a flag in a simplified form, e.g. with just the shield.

***Banner:*** A flag bearing a coat of arms, or hung from a crossbar, or between two poles. Figuratively it refers to any type of flag.

***Battle honour:*** An inscription on military colours designed to show the particular successes of a unit in combat.

***Bicolour:*** A flag of two bands of colour, arranged horizontally or vertically, e.g. Monaco.

***Bunting:*** A type of plain weave material used in the manufacture of flags. Also a string of decorative small flags.

***Burgee:*** A triangular or swallowtail flag used by ships, notably yachts to show membership of a particular yacht club.

***Canton:*** A quarter of the area of a flag or shield; refers particularly to the quarter in the upper left corner.

**Charge:** A figure or symbol in the field of a flag or a shield.

**Civil flag:** A national flag used by private citizens on land. In this book, state flags are illustrated as the main picture with the civil flag or flag of sovreignty (where appropriate) shown in the left- or right-hand corner (see How to Use on pages 22–3).

**Coat of arms:** See **Arms.**

**Colours:** The flag of a military unit, such as a regiment. Metaphorically speaking, it also refers to the flag of a country.

**Counterchange:** To reverse two colours on either side of a line on a flag, e.g. in the crosses of St Andrew and St Patrick on the Union Jack.

**Device:** Anything placed on the field of the flag as a distinctive marking. This may be a badge, but could also be a circle, triangle or block of stripes.

**Dexter:** On the right-hand side of a shield or flag as seen from a bearer's viewpoint, so on the left-hand side as seen by a viewer.

**Emblem:** A device often used as a charge on a flag but which can also be used separately. It is used to represent a nation, city, family or an idea. It may be of heraldic origin or more modern, e.g. the maple leaf on the Canadian flag.

**Ensign:** A national flag flown at the stern of a ship. A country may have a civil ensign (for civil and merchant ships), state ensign (for non-military vessels) and naval ensign (for warships).

**Field:** The background of a flag or a shield.

**Fimbriation:** A narrow edging or border, often in white or yellow, to separate two other colours on a flag.

**Flag:** A decorated piece of cloth, usually attached to a pole or staff, used for identification, symbolizing, signalling, etc.

**Flag of convenience:** A flag of a particular country flown by a foreign ship registered there to take advantage of that country's weaker financial or legal regulations.

**Fly:** The outer edge of a flag; usually referring to the half furthest away from the flagpole.

**Half-mast:** Flying a flag below the top of a flagpole to show mourning. A romantic invention of the late 19th century, flying the flag at half-mast left room above for the 'Flag of Death'.

**Hoist:** The edge of a flag nearest the flagpole; usually referring to the half nearest the pole. The verb hoist means to raise a flag.

**International Code:** A means of signalling with flags representing specific letters of the alphabet.

**Jack:** A small flag flown at a ship's bow to show nationality.

**Jolly Roger:** A flag traditionally used by pirates and comprising a white skull above two crossed bones set on a black field.

**Length:** The measurement of a flag along the side at right angles to the flagpole.

**Obverse:** The more important side of a flag, visible when the flagpole is on the viewer's left.

**National flag:** See **Civil flag, State flag**.

**Pennant:** A small tapering or triangular flag, used especially on ships for identification or signalling; also used as a souvenir or decoration.

**Rank flag:** A flag, generally used in the armed forces, to show the status of an officer.

**Ratio:** A flag's proportions described as relative width to length.

**Reverse:** The less important side of a flag, seen when the flagpole is on the observer's right.

**Semaphore:** A means of signalling by holding a flag in each hand and moving the arms to designated positions representing letters of the alphabet.

**Sinister:** On the left-hand side of a shield or flag as seen from a bearer's viewpoint, so on the right-hand side as seen by a viewer.

**Standard:** A flag of any kind, including a vexilloid, medieval banner, heraldic or military flag, or personal banner.

**State flag:** The national flag flown on land by government offices, military establishments and overseas diplomatic buildings. It is also used to represent the country overseas, e.g. at the Olympics. Where these differ from civil flags, they normally carry the national arms. The main flags illustrated throughout this book are state flags (with civil flags illustrated in the top left- or right-hand corner – see How to Use on page 22–3).

**Swallowtail:** A flag with a triangular portion cut out of the fly. One with a double triangular cut is called a swallowtail with tongue. This style of flag is used in the ensigns of Scandinavian countries.

**Tribar:** A flag of two colours in three stripes, arranged either horizontally or vertically, e.g. Austria and Nigeria.

**Tricolour:** A flag of three bands of different colour which are arranged horizontally or vertically, e.g. France.

**Vexilloid:** An emblem, either solid (such as the standard of a Roman legion) or cloth (such as a flag).

**Vexillology:** The study of flags and their history.

**Width:** The measurement of a flag down the side parallel to the flagpole.

# HOW TO USE THIS BOOK

In this book we have illustrated the state flag in the main image. The corner flag shows the civil flag or sovereignty flag (where applicable).

The state flag is the national flag which is flown on land by government offices, military establishments and overseas diplomatic buildings. It is also used to represent the country overseas, e.g. at the Olympics.

The civil flag is the national flag which can be used by private citizens on land. Sometimes both state and civil flags are the same. Sometimes a coat of arms or emblem is added to the state flag.

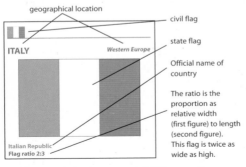

geographical location

civil flag

**ITALY**                          *Western Europe*

state flag

Official name of country

The ratio is the proportion as relative width (first figure) to length (second figure). This flag is twice as wide as high.

Italian Republic
Flag ratio 2:3

In this example both state and civil flags are the same.

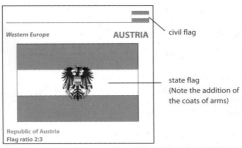

civil flag

state flag
(Note the addition of
the coats of arms)

In this example the state flag differs from the civil flag.

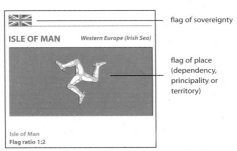

flag of sovereignty

flag of place
(dependency,
principality or
territory)

In this example the corner flag indicates that the
Isle of Man flag does not have national status and
that the Isle of Man comes under the sovereignty of
the United Kingdom.

# AFGHANISTAN

*Southern Asia*

**Islamic State of Afghanistan**
**Flag ratio 1:2**
Afghanistan had a troubled history in the late 20th century. In 1974, the kingdom was overthrown, followed by years of civil war and foreign intervention, which wrecked the country. There was also the successive adoption of six different flags, as different rulers took control. The present flag was adopted in 2002. It closely resembles the pre-1974 royal flag. The earlier flag emblem was white and differed in inscriptions from the present design. When the colours were adopted in 1928, black was for the Abbasid caliphate, under which Afghanistan became a Muslim country. Red was for royalty and green for Islam itself. These came to be regarded as traditional Afghan colours and have appeared on most flags since then.

*Scandinavia*     # ÅLAND ISLANDS

**Åland Islands**
**Flag ratio 17:26**

The Åland Islands belong to Finland, but are mainly
Swedish in language. Both these national traditions
are honoured in the islands' flag. It has the pattern
and colours of the flag of Sweden, with the addition
of a red cross, red and yellow being the colours of the
arms of Finland.

# ALBANIA

*Eastern Europe*

**Republic of Albania**
**Flag ratio 5:7**
The symbol of the two-headed black eagle which
appears on the red field of the Albanian flag echoes
the flag of Skanderbeg, the 15th-century leader
against the Turkish invasion of the country. The word
'Albania' means 'Land of the Eagle'. This emblem also
represented the Byzantine Empire of the 5th–15th
centuries, of which Albania was part. A yellow-
fimbriated red star, symbol of Communism, was
added by the Communist government after World
War II. When Communism was abandoned in 1992,
the star was removed from the flag.

*North Africa*

# ALGERIA

**People's Democratic Republic of Algeria**
**Flag ratio 2:3**

The flag of Algeria was officially adopted when the country gained independence from France in 1962. Conflicting stories exist to explain its origins: traditionally it was said to have been used by patriots fighting French colonisation in the early 19th century. But it is now thought more likely that it was designed for the National Liberation Movement (Front de Libération National) in 1928, being used in the struggle for independence from then on. The green of the hoist is the traditional colour of Islam; white in the fly represents purity; and the red crescent and star over them are recognised emblems of Islam, their colour symbolising the blood of national heroes.

# AMERICAN SAMOA

*Pacific Ocean*

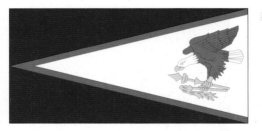

**Territory of American Samoa**

**Flag ratio 1:2**

The eastern part of the archipelago of Samoa was a dependency of the United States of America from 1899, and achieved self-government as an overseas territory in 1960. The flag was adopted in the same year. The American bald eagle clutching a chief's staff and a knife, traditional Samoan symbols of authority, signifies American protection of Samoa. The colours against which this motif appears – blue, red and white – are the colours of the American flag.

*Western Europe*

# ANDORRA

**Principality of Andorra**
**Flag ratio 2:3**
Said to be based on the French tricolour, Andorra's flag was adopted in 1866. The principality has been under Franco–Spanish suzerainty since 1278, with the flag's colours indicating its protectors. The Andorran coat of arms in the centre comprise a quartered shield showing the arms of its two traditional protectors and joint princes, the Spanish bishops of Urgel (represented by a mitre and crozier) and the French counts of Foix (three stripes of red on yellow), as well as the arms of Catalonia (four red stripes on yellow) and of Béarn (two cows). A motto, *Virtus Unita Fortior* ('United Strength is Greater'), appears at the base.

# ANGOLA

*Southern Africa*

**Republic of Angola**
**Flag ratio 2:3**

The national flag, adopted in 1975, was based on the flag of the MPLA (Movimiento Popular de Libertação de Angola), the main nationalist group who won the country's independence after centuries as a Portuguese colony. The MPLA formed the new government and used parts of its flag as a basis for the national one: its colours – red, signifying the struggle for liberty and blood shed in the fight, and black for Africa – and its star, which represents Communism and internationalism. The half gear wheel and machete, local variations on the hammer and sickle of the old Soviet flag, stand for industry and agriculture. The central motif's yellow colour represents the country's wealth.

*Caribbean*

# ANGUILLA

## Colony of Anguilla
**Flag ratio 1:2**

Anguilla was linked with St Kitts and Nevis until 1967. In that year, during preparations for independence, Anguilla broke away to become a British colony in its own right. At the time, an unofficial flag was designed. This showed a circle of three orange dolphins for strength, unity and endurance on a white band for peace. A light blue band crossed the bottom of the flag to symbolise youthfulness and hope. In 1990, this design was adapted for the island's coat of arms. The arms now appear in the fly of a British Blue Ensign to form the official colonial flag (main image). The unofficial flag is still used on land.

# ANTIGUA AND BARBUDA    *Caribbean*

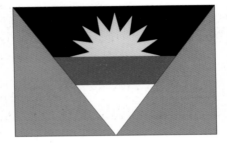

**Antigua and Barbuda**
**Flag ratio 2:3**
A competition held when Antigua and Barbuda
became an associated state in 1967, prior to full
independence from Britain, decided the look of the
islands' flag. The winning entry comprised two outer
triangles of red, to express the vigour and dynamism
of the people, with the golden sun of a new era rising
over three stripes of black (signifying both the soil
and the people's African heritage), blue (representing
hope) and white. The bands' arrangement with the
red triangles forms a 'V' shape, the symbol of victory.
This design also promotes the islands' attractions –
sun, sea and sand (gold, blue and white). The flag
continued in use after independence in 1981.

*South America*

# ARGENTINA

**Argentine Republic**
**Flag ratio 1:2**
The Argentinian colours were identified with the fight
for freedom from Spain, and greatly influenced other
flags in the region. Manuel Belgrano's Liberation Army
wore blue and white cockades to distinguish them from
Spanish troops, as both had red insignias. On 25 May
1810, when crowds in Buenos Aires demanded
independence they also wore the cockades, and the
colours were later used in the national flag. The yellow
Sun of May, in the centre of the state flag, was taken
from the sun depicted on the first gold coins minted
by the new government in 1810. It was said to represent
both the sun as it appeared on 25 May and the
bright future for the new nation.

# ARMENIA

*Eastern Europe*

**Republic of Armenia**
**Flag ratio 1:2**
Armenia's flag was adopted in 1990, a year before the break-up of the USSR, of which it was part. Armenia had been independent from 1918 until 1921, after the collapse of the Russian Empire and before the USSR came into being. Red is for the struggles against the Turks. Blue is for the unchanged character of the land. Orange represents courage and the work of the people. These colours were used in banners of the region as long ago as the 2nd century BC. Like many other former Soviet republics, Armenia kept the 1:2 ratio of the old Soviet flag rather than the 2:3 ratio of the flag of 1918–21.

*Caribbean*

# ARUBA

**Autonomous Dutch Territory of Aruba**

**Flag ratio 2:3**

Formerly part of the Netherlands Antilles, Aruba separated from other islands in the group in 1986. It is now a self-governing possession of the Netherlands. The flag dates from 1976. The blue field represents the Caribbean Sea. The red, four-pointed, white-fimbriated star in the canton stands for progress and is red to link with the Netherlands flag. The two yellow stripes near the lower edge symbolise Aruba's independence, yet closeness to its Caribbean neighbours, and also mean its golden beaches and future prosperity.

# AUSTRALIA

*Australasia*

**Commonwealth of Australia**
**Flag ratio 1:2**
The use of a British Blue Ensign marks Australia as
a former British colony. It was adopted in 1901 on
unification of the country. The Union Flag shows
continuing links with Britain. The Commonwealth
Star of seven points under the Union Flag is for the
union of the six states and the territories of Australia.
In the fly is a representation of the Southern Cross
constellation, very prominent in the Australian sky.
The Aboriginal people also have a flag. It is equal
horizontal stripes of black over red with a large gold
sun in the centre. It shows the black Aboriginal
people, living on the red land under the golden sun
(see Introduction, page 10).

*Western Europe* **AUSTRIA**

**Republic of Austria**

**Flag ratio 2:3**

The red, white, red tribar has been Austria's national colours since the Battle of Acre in 1191, when (according to legend) the white tunic of Leopold V of Babenberg was so bloody that the only part still white was the part under his sword-belt. The state flag (main image) has the arms of the republic in the centre, a black imperial eagle extending into both red bands, with the colours in a shield on its chest. The hammer, sickle and turreted crown represent industry, agriculture and commerce. When Austria was made part of Germany in 1938, the flag was not used. When Austrian independence was restored in 1945, broken chains were added to the eagle's feet to symbolise Austria's liberty.

# AZERBAIJAN

*Eastern Europe*

**Republic of Azerbaijan**
**Flag ratio 1:2**

Azerbaijan's tricolour was adopted in 1991 at the break-up of the USSR, of which the country was a part. The flag's colours are symbolic: blue shows Azerbaijani ethnic affinity with the Turkic peoples (who use this colour in their flags); red is for the development of culture in Azerbaijan; and green stands for the Muslim religion. As in other states where most people are Muslim, Azerbaijan uses the familiar Islamic crescent and star symbols on its flag, and the star's eight points represent the eight groupings within the Turkic peoples. The flag was adopted originally in 1918 and was the national flag until Bolshevik forces occupied the country in 1920.

*Caribbean*

# BAHAMAS

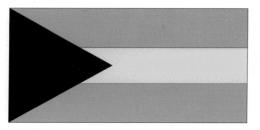

**Commonwealth of the Bahamas**

**Flag ratio 1:2**

Now a member of the British Commonwealth, the Bahamas were formerly a British colony, gaining both independence and a new national flag in 1973. The flag's design was based on the winning entry in a competition and represents the qualities of the islands and their people: the aquamarine blue, yellow and aquamarine blue bands symbolise the islands' physical location and attributes, as sandy islands in an archipelago, surrounded by water. The black triangle in the hoist reflects the unity and vigour of the people.

# BAHRAIN

*Middle East*

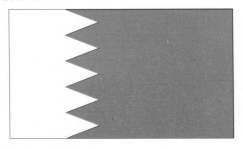

**Kingdom of Bahrain**
**Flag ratio 3:5**

Bahrain, an archipelago in the Arabian Gulf, was under British protection from 1820 until 1971, when independence was gained. Red was the colour of the Kharijite Muslims in eastern Arabia. In the treaty of 1820, Britain asked all friendly states in the area to add white to their flags. White would show that the ship was not a pirate. Piracy was a problem in the Gulf, and Britain wanted to protect her shipping routes. The flag dates from 1932, when the edge between the colours was made serrated. In 2002 the number of serrations was reduced to five.

*Southern Asia* # BANGLADESH

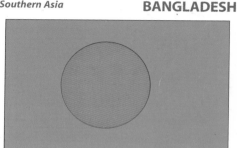

**People's Republic of Bangladesh**
**Flag ratio 3:5**

The Bangladeshi national flag was adopted in 1971, when the country (formerly East Pakistan) gained its independence from West Pakistan. The green of the field represents the fertility of the land and the youth and vigour of the country, as well as reflecting the importance of the Islamic religion. The red circle symbolises the national struggle for freedom, being the sun of independence rising after the dark night of a bloody struggle. A map of the country initially appeared in the circle, but this was dropped within a few months. The red circle, which seems to be in the centre, is actually set slightly towards the hoist so it can be seen more clearly as the flag flutters.

# BARBADOS

*Caribbean*

**Barbados**
**Flag ratio 2:3**
Like the flags of some other Caribbean nations,
the flag of Barbados was the result of a competition
to find a suitable emblem. Like many too, it stresses
the favoured geographical situation of the island.
A vertical tribar of blue, gold, blue shows Barbados'
gold beaches in the blue waters of the Caribbean.
The trident of the sea-god, Neptune, appeared on
the colonial arms. Now the broken shaft on the gold
shows the island has broken away to independence,
while still respecting the traditions of the past. It shows
Barbados' status as an independent state since gaining
its freedom from Britain in 1966.

*Eastern Europe*

# BELARUS

**Republic of Belarus**
**Flag ratio 1:2**
With the official break-up of the USSR in 1991,
Byelorussia (as Belarus was then known) adopted a
white, red, white tribar as its flag. This was based on
one it had used during a short time of independence
between 1918 and 1920. A new flag was introduced
in 1995, featuring a traditional ornament of
Belarussian design in the hoist. This is a modified
form of what appeared on the former Soviet flag of
the country, from which the red and green colours
also derive.

# BELGIUM

*Western Europe*

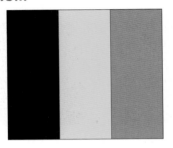

**Kingdom of Belgium**
**Flag ratio 13:15**
The colours in this flag were first used in 1789,
a year of revolutionary unrest in Europe, when Belgium
fought to free itself from rule by the Hapsburgs'
Austro-Hungarian Empire. The colours were said to
derive from the arms of the province of Brabant, one
of the foremost provinces, although the same colours
feature in the arms of most Belgian provinces.
The bands were arranged horizontally until 1830,
when Belgium finally became independent; the new
vertical pattern followed that of the French tricolour,
although the flag retained the almost square shape
it had when carried into battle against the Dutch in
1830.

*Central America*                    **BELIZE**

**Belize**
**Flag ratio 2:3**
Formerly British Honduras, Belize adopted an unofficial
flag when it became self-governing in 1964. This was
the basis for the flag adopted at independence in 1981.
The national arms in the centre date from the
early 19th century but were not recognised until 1907.
The shield's top panels show traditional tools used in
logging, once the main industry. Below is a sailing ship,
for trade. The supporters are a mestizo and a creole
worker and above is a mahogany tree, national tree
and main resource. Below is the motto *Sub Umbra
Floreo* ('I Flourish in the Shade'). It was associated with
the People's United Party, so balancing bands of red,
for the rival United Democratic Party, were added.

# BENIN

*West Africa*

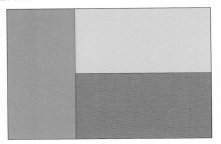

**Republic of Benin**
**Flag ratio 2:3**

Dahomey, as Benin was previously known, was a colony of France and, in common with many other African states, adopted the red, yellow and green colours of the Pan-African movement, expressive of African unity and nationalism, on independence in 1960. The colours were adapted to two horizontal bands of yellow over red, with a green band in the hoist. The flag was changed in 1975 under the Communist government (when the country's name also changed, to Benin) to a plain green field with a red Communist star in the canton, but with the collapse of single-party rule in August 1991, the flag was changed back again to its original design.

*Caribbean*

# BERMUDA

**Colony of Bermuda**

**Flag ratio 1:2**

One of the oldest British colonies, Bermuda was first settled in 1609, after British ships, led by the *Sea Venture*, were wrecked off the coast en route to Virginia (an event which may have inspired Shakespeare's 1611 play, *The Tempest*). A shield for the island's coat of arms was drawn up soon after, and remains in use today. A red lion holds a shield in which the *Sea Venture* is seen foundering on coastal rocks. The arms were officially adopted in 1910, the 300th anniversary of the establishment of the colony, and placed in the fly of a British Red Ensign to form the colonial flag. Only Canada and Bermuda chose to use the Red, rather than the Blue Ensign on land.

# BHUTAN

*Southern Asia*

**Kingdom of Bhutan**
**Flag ratio 2:3**

The design of this flag was adopted in the 1960s, when Bhutan became a member state of the United Nations. In the local Tibetan dialect, Bhutan's name is Druk Yul, 'Land of the Dragon'. Coincidentally, *druk* also means 'thunder', explaining the local myth that the noise of thunder in the Himalayas was the roaring of dragons among the peaks. Bhutan's dragon represents the nation, although the dragon is also a symbol throughout the Orient of benevolence and power. The two colours on the flag, divided diagonally, represent temporal and spiritual power: the lower portion, flame-red, stands for Buddhist spiritual authority, while the upper portion of saffron is for royal authority.

*South America* **BOLIVIA**

**Republic of Bolivia**
**Flag ratio 2:3**
The Bolivian tricolour was adopted after independence in 1825–6. The present design dates from 1851. Red symbolises national valour and the blood shed for independence. Yellow is for mineral resources, and green for agricultural wealth. The state flag (main image) has arms which are oval and show emblems of the country's agricultural, mining and wildlife resources. The border has the name and nine stars for the nine provinces. Above is the national bird, the Andean condor, and a trophy of flags and weapons surrounds the design. Without the arms the plain tricolour is the flag used by citizens. When not appearing on the flag, the arms are shown on a blue circle.

# BOSNIA AND HERZEGOVINA

*Eastern Europe*

**Republic of Bosnia and Herzegovina**
**Flag ratio 1:2**

Bosnia and Herzegovina has only recently regained independence after centuries of rule by outsiders. In 1992 it seceded from the crumbling Yugoslavia but with the country's three ethnic groups – Muslims, Serbs and Croats – at war, a neutral flag of white with a central blue, white and gold shield of the last independent 14th-century king was chosen. This became identified with the Muslims and a new design was needed. As the factions could not agree, in 1998 the International High Representative chose the present flag. The old colours were reused, with the triangle echoing the country's shape and its three ethnic groups. The stars, based on the EU flag, are for peace and the future.

*Southern Africa*

# BOTSWANA

**Republic of Botswana**
**Flag ratio 2:3**

The national flag of Botswana was adopted when the protectorate gained its independence from Britain in 1966. It comprises a horizontal black stripe, fimbriated in white, across a blue field. The colours on the flag correspond to those on the national coat of arms. The blue represents water, of vital importance in this largely arid land whose main industries are animal husbandry and agriculture (the motto on the national arms is Pula, meaning 'Let there be rain'). The white–black–white bands depict the racial harmony of the people as well as the pluralist nature of society. They are inspired by the coat of the zebra, the national animal.

# BRAZIL

*South America*

**Federative Republic of Brazil**
**Flag ratio 7:10**

This flag's colours have been used since 1822, when the Crown Prince of Portugal, fleeing Napoleonic Europe, declared Brazil independent. The green field shows Brazil's rainforests and the yellow diamond its mineral resources, especially gold. The sphere depicts the stellar constellations over Rio de Janeiro. The stars represent the Brazilian states and Federal District. The band reads *Ordem e Progresso* ('Order and Progress') and the whole central emblem replaces the royal arms which were dropped in 1889, when the monarchy was overthrown. The idea of using a globe may have come from earlier flags which featured a crowned armillary sphere, an instrument used by early navigators.

*Indian Ocean*

# BRITISH INDIAN OCEAN TERRITORY

**British Indian Ocean Territory**
**Flag ratio 1:2**
The flag of the British Indian Ocean Territory was approved in November 1990. Its blue and white wavy stripes represent the waters of the Indian Ocean. The palm tree stands for the islands themselves, while the crown over the tree and the Union Flag in the canton indicate its status as a British territory.

# BRITISH VIRGIN ISLANDS   *Caribbean*

**Colony of the British Virgin Islands**
**Flag ratio 1:2**
The Virgin Islands are shared between Britain and the
US. They were discovered by Columbus in 1493, and
settled by the British in 1666, after being under Spanish
and Dutch control. The colonial flag (main image)
is the British Blue Ensign with the badge in the fly.
This is a green shield with a woman in white holding
a lamp. Eleven more lamps are around her. The islands'
name comes from their discovery on the feast of the
5th-century virgin martyr, St Ursula. She was reputedly
killed in a Roman persecution of Christians, along
with 11,000 companions. This is the origin of the
lamps. The motto *Vigilate* ('Be vigilant') is on a scroll
below the shield.

*Eastern Asia*

# BRUNEI

**Brunei Darussalam**
**Flag ratio 1:2**
The flag of Brunei has evolved gradually throughout
this century. Its base, a plain yellow field, was the flag
of the sultan, its ruler. To this were added in 1906
two diagonal stripes, a broad one of white over a
narrower of black, in recognition of British protection.
The state arms were added in 1959. A crescent, a
traditional symbol of Islam, bears words meaning
'Always Give Service by God's Guidance'. The motto
below reads 'Brunei, City of Peace'. The arms on either
side are upraised to God.

# BULGARIA

*Eastern Europe*

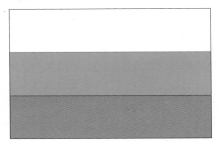

**Republic of Bulgaria**
**Flag ratio 2:3**
The colours of the Bulgarian flag are both symbolic in themselves and representative of the 19th-century Pan-Slav nationalist movement. As the Slav communities of Eastern Europe tried to pull away from the Hapsburg Empire, so they fell under the influence of imperial Russia, and the Pan-Slav flags tended to use the Russian white, blue and red tricolour as a model. However, green was used in place of blue in the Bulgarian flag, designed in 1878, both to distinguish it from the Russian and Slovenian flags, which were identical, and to express the youthfulness of the emergent nation. White is said to represent a love of peace, and red symbolises the valour of the people.

*West Africa* **BURKINA FASO**

Burkina Faso
**Flag ratio 2:3**

When Burkina Faso gained independence from
France in 1960 it took the name Upper Volta, derived
from a river whose source lay within its borders.
The colours from the names of its tributaries – Black,
White and Red Volta – were given to the horizontal
tricolour adopted as the national flag. The country's
name and flag were both changed in 1984 in what
was intended to be a deliberate turning away from its
colonial past and an identification with the concerns
of its own continent. The colours of the Pan-African
movement, representing aspirations towards African
unity, were adopted: two bands of red over green,
with yellow in the form of a central star.

# BURUNDI

*Central Africa*

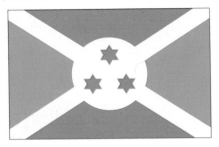

**Republic of Burundi**
**Flag ratio 2:3**

In common with many former colonies, Burundi celebrates its independence on its flag. The white saltire expresses a desire for peace. Red above and below commemorates the struggle for independence from colonial rule. Green at the hoist and fly expresses hope for the future. The three red stars fimbriated green in the white circle are for the words of the national motto, 'Unity, Work, Progress'. The flag was adopted at independence in 1962, showing a plant and a drum in the centre. These emblems of monarchy were removed in 1967 when the monarchy was overthrown and a republic installed.

*Eastern Asia* # CAMBODIA

**Kingdom of Cambodia**
**Flag ratio 2:3**

The flag of Cambodia has always featured a
representation of the 12th-century Angkor Wat temple,
the country's most famous monument, although the
colours in the field have varied slightly. The United
Nations supervised the settlement of the country's
civil war and it is now a constitutional monarchy.
The latest form of its flag, which is particularly
associated with the new king, Prince Sihanouk,
was introduced in June 1993. This flag was originally
introduced in 1948 and was used up to the founding
of the Khmer Republic in 1970.

# CAMEROON

*West Africa*

**Republic of Cameroon**
**Flag ratio 2:3**

The Pan-African colours, representing aspirations towards African unity, are arranged in the style of the French tricolour to form the basis of the Cameroon flag. Until 1960–61, the country was split in two parts, administered by France and Britain. The French part was the first to achieve independence in 1960, and the tricolour had been used as a model for the green, red and yellow flag which had been adopted three years before. When the British sector joined the rest the next year, two vertically arranged yellow stars were added to the canton to reflect the two parts of the country. In 1972 these were replaced by a single yellow star in the centre to show national unity.

*North America*

# CANADA

Canada
**Flag ratio 1:2**
The distinctive red and white flag of Canada was adopted in 1965 after efforts to find an emblem which would be acceptable to all citizens. The Red Ensign, with the Canadian arms in the fly, was in use from 1892 to 1921, when the arms were updated. The flag remained unpopular with many, particularly the French community. Red and white, as used in the Canadian Red Ensign and in the coat of arms, were the national colours, and they were used in the new flag: a white, full-depth central square with a red band down either side. In the white square is a large red maple leaf, a Canadian emblem from the 18th century.

# CAPE VERDE  *West Africa (N Atlantic Ocean)*

**Republic of Cape Verde**
**Flag ratio 2:3**
Cape Verde adopted a new flag after changing its
constitution in 1992. The country gained independence
from Portugal in 1975, and its then flag was modelled
on that of Guinea-Bissau, with whom it was in a loose
federation. As in many former African colonies, the
green–red–yellow Pan-African colours were used.
The federation ended in 1980 and in 1992, with the
end of one-party rule, the present flag was adopted.
The ten stars are for the ten islands comprising the
country. The blue field is for the sea. The stripes show
the road to national development, white for willing-
ness and peace and red for effort and determination.

*Caribbean*

# CAYMAN ISLANDS

**Colony of the Cayman Islands**
**Flag ratio 1:2**

The Cayman Islands were colonised by Britain, but administered by Jamaica until 1962. With Jamaican independence that year, they reverted to being a British colony. The flag is the British Blue Ensign, with the islands' arms, granted in 1958. The shield has a gold English heraldic lion on red in the chief (upper part). Blue and white wavy lines below represent the sea, and the three green, yellow-fimbriated stars are for the islands in the group. The crest shows a coil of rope, which the islands once exported, with a local species of turtle and a pineapple to show the past link with Jamaica. Below is a scroll with the motto 'He Hath Founded it Upon the Seas'.

# CENTRAL AFRICAN REPUBLIC

*Central Africa*

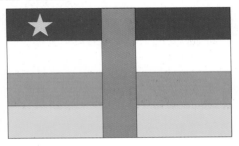

**Central African Republic**

**Flag ratio 3:5**

The desire for harmony and cooperation between the Central African Republic and its former coloniser, France, as well as for African unity, is expressed in the unusual design of this flag which was adopted in 1958, two years before the country gained independence. Its colours symbolise ideals, including freedom (blue), equality and purity (white), hope (green) and tolerance (yellow). The red, crossing the other four colours, represents both national heroes and unity. The colours of France and the Pan-African movement, with its ideal of African unity, are both present. The five-pointed gold star in the blue of the canton expresses further the hope of African unity.

*Central Africa* **CHAD**

**Republic of Chad**
**Flag ratio 2:3**
The flag of the Republic of Chad, adopted the year before the country became independent of France in 1960, is based on the French tricolour, with yellow replacing white. This gives two of France's colours and two Pan-African colours. The colours have been given new meanings. Blue is for the sky and the water of the south. Yellow represents the sun and the northern desert. Red is for valour and sacrifice in the struggle for freedom.

# CHILE

*South America*

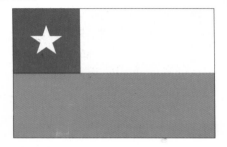

**Republic of Chile**
**Flag ratio 2:3**
As the French flag was a model for the flags of
emergent European nations stressing the ideals of
progress and revolution, so was the American flag in
the New World. The Chilean flag's colours were based
on the Stars and Stripes, and it was adopted in 1817
during the struggle for freedom from Spain. Initially
a horizontal tricolour of blue, white and red, the design
was modified in 1854 to the present layout: two
horizontal bands of white over red, with a blue canton
charged with a white star. The white band depicts the
snow of the Andes, the blue the sky, the red the blood
of patriots who died in the fight for independence,
and the white star is a symbol of progress.

*Eastern Asia*

# CHINA

**People's Republic of China**
**Flag ratio 2:3**
The five-star red flag of the People's Republic of China was officially adopted in 1949 on the day the republic was founded. The red field uses a colour associated with both China and revolution. The large gold star in the canton represents the Common Programme of the Communist Party, while the four smaller stars symbolise the social classes it unites: workers, peasants, petty bourgeois and capitalists sympathetic to the party. Collectively, the five stars symbolise the people's unity under the Communist Party. The flags used by the old Kuomintang (Chinese Nationalist Party) government until the establishment of the People's Republic, are now used in Taiwan.

# COLOMBIA

*South America*

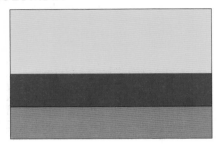

**Republic of Colombia**
**Flag ratio 2:3**
This flag, like those of Colombia's neighbours Ecuador and Venezuela, is based on that flown by the armies of Simón Bolívar during his rebellion against Spanish rule. The flag was originally used by Bolívar's predecessor, Francisco de Miranda, in 1806. The flag continued to be used by Colombia even after Ecuador and Venezuela finally broke away from what was then Gran Colombia in 1830. Today, the colours are said to represent the following: yellow or gold, for Colombia's natural riches; blue, for the sky and seas surrounding Colombia; and red, for the blood shed by the freedom fighters during the struggle for independence from Spain.

*Southern Africa (Indian Ocean)*   **COMOROS**

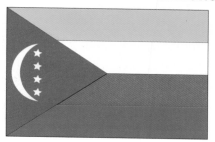

**Union of the Comoros**

**Flag ratio 3:5**

On independence from France in 1975, the Comoro Islands adopted a flag which showed their Muslim faith and the legacy of their conquest by Arabs. Although it was adapted several times in later years, the flag remained essentially the same, green with a white crescent and four stars for the four islands. In 2002 the flag was given its present form. The white crescent and stars on green remain, as a triangle in the hoist. The horizontal stripes of yellow, white, red and blue represent the islands, as do the stars.

# CONGO

*Central Africa*

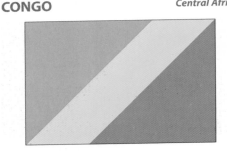

**Republic of the Congo**
**Flag ratio 2:3**
The original flag of the Congo was restored in 1991
after being out of use for 21 years. The green–yellow–
red diagonal design was in use from independence
from France in 1960, until 1970, when a Communist
government replaced it. The new flag was based on
that of the USSR – red with local tools for agriculture
and industry crossed in the canton under a star.
The colours remained the same, to express continued
solidarity with other African states. A change of
government restored the original independence flag.
The Congo is unofficially called Congo-Brazzaville
(after its capital), to distinguish it from the Democratic
Republic of Congo (Congo-Kinshasa).

*Pacific Ocean* # COOK ISLANDS

## Cook Islands
**Flag ratio 1:2**

These islands were named after Captain James Cook, although they were discovered almost 200 years before he visited them in the late 18th century. They were administered by New Zealand from 1901 to 1965, when they became a self-governing dependency (note New Zealand corner flag). The basis of the islands' flag is the Blue Ensign, emphasising indirectly their links with the Commonwealth through New Zealand. In the fly is a ring of 15 five-pointed stars, representing the 15 islands in the group. The choice of stars as a design feature is something which the Cook Islands have in common with other Pacific island countries.

# COSTA RICA

*Central America*

**Republic of Costa Rica**
**Flag ratio 3:5**
Costa Rica's flag reflects its membership of the
United Provinces of Central America (1823–38), like
co-members El Salvador, Guatemala, Nicaragua and
Honduras. It was adopted in 1821 at independence,
and the red stripe was added in 1848 when the
country finally secured independence as a republic.
The red distinguished it from the other Central
American flags and honoured revolutionary France.
The state flag has the national arms in a white oval
set towards the hoist: ships on the Caribbean and
Pacific, separated by Costa Rica. A rising sun is for the
new era and the stars represent the seven provinces.
'America Central' recalls the United Provinces.

*West Africa*

# CÔTE D'IVOIRE

**Republic of Côte d'Ivoire**
**Flag ratio 2:3**

A French colony from the late 19th century until 1960, the Ivory Coast is another country which based its flag on the French tricolour. The colours are said to represent progress and the northern plains, or savannah (orange); hope and the agriculture of the south (green); and national unity (white). Coincidentally and significantly, green and white are also the colours of the Parti Démocratique de la Côte d'Ivoire (Ivory Coast Democratic Party), which led the country to independence and has subsequently banned all rival political opposition. The Ivory Coast flag is similar to that of Ireland, but with the colours reversed and with different proportions.

# CROATIA

*Eastern Europe*

**Republic of Croatia**

**Flag ratio 1:2**

All the Slavic territories of the Austro-Hungarian Empire were part of the 19th-century Pan-Slav movement for self-rule. In 1848 the Slavs sought Russian support and almost all, including Croatia, adopted flags based on Russia's tricolour. The southern Slav states, Croatia being one, were united into a new country, Yugoslavia, in 1919, but there were rivalries between the different parts. When Yugoslavia broke up in 1992, Croatia and Slovenia left the union. Croatia re-adopted its earlier flag, a red, white and blue tricolour, with the arms in the centre. This is a shield of red and white checks. Above is an arch of the traditional arms of Croatia Ancient, Dubrovnik, Dalmatia, Istria and Slavonia, all parts of Croatia.

*Caribbean*

# CUBA

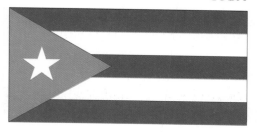

**Republic of Cuba**
**Flag ratio 1:2**
The flag of Cuba, designed in 1849, was influenced
in design and colour by the flags of the US and France,
then regarded as revolutionary in outlook and
aspiration. The three horizontal blue stripes stand
for Cuba's three provinces from the mid-19th century,
and the two white stripes show the purity of Cuban
ideals. The red triangle in the hoist is a symbol of
the sacrifice of the people struggling to gain their
independence from the Spanish Empire, while the
white star indicates Cuba's status as a free and
independent nation. The flag was adopted by the
independence movement of 1868–69, and was
retained as the national flag after independence
was achieved fully in 1902.

# CYPRUS

*Eastern Europe*

**Republic of Cyprus**
**Flag ratio 2:3**
In view of the hostilities which took place after its adoption, the Cypriot flag is a poignant symbol of attempts to unite the island's Greek and Turkish communities. Use of blue and red, colours of Greece and Turkey, was deliberately avoided; instead, the adoption of both the white field and crossed olive branches symbolises a desire for ethnic peace, white also being a neutral colour between the two. A map of Cyprus appears in orange, recalling the rich copper deposits for which the island was famous in ancient times. The flag came into use when the island became independent from Britain in 1960, and it may be flown with the Greek and Turkish flags on public holidays.

77

*Eastern Europe*  # CZECH REPUBLIC

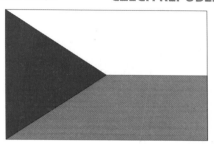

**Czech Republic**
**Flag ratio 2:3**
The Czech flag dates back to 1920, two years after independence at the end of World War I. The new country, known as Czechoslovakia, was formed of three states, Bohemia, Moravia and Slovakia, so the flag had to express unity. The basis is the white and red of Bohemia, with the blue of Moravia added as a triangle. When Czechoslovakia was broken up before World War II, the flag was abolished, but it was reinstated when the country regained freedom in 1945. Although Czechs and Slovaks had been involved in the Pan-Slav movement, the link between the Russian and Czech colours is coincidence. When Czechoslovakia split into two countries in 1993, the Czech Republic retained the traditional flag.

# DEMOCRATIC REPUBLIC OF CONGO

*Central Africa*

**Democratic Republic of Congo**

**Flag ratio 2:3**

The Democratic Republic of Congo has had three flags since it gained independence from Belgium in 1960. The first was the same as the present one, and was based on an earlier colonial flag of a gold star on blue, showing the light of hope shining in Africa. On independence, six stars were added along the hoist for the six provinces. The country suffered from civil wars and secession. It reunited in 1971 with the name Zaïre, and a new flag in the Pan-African colours. When the government was deposed in 1996, the original name of the country and its first post-independence flag were restored.

*Scandinavia* # DENMARK

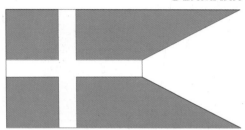

**Kingdom of Denmark**
**Flag ratio 28:34**
The flag of Denmark, the Dannebrog, may have originated earlier than any other national flag. According to legend, the white cross on red was given as a sign to the crusader King Valdemar II of Denmark, before the Battle of Lyndanisse against the pagan Estonians in 1219. The distinctive off-centre cross with the upright set towards the hoist was used as a model by other Scandinavian countries, some of which were ruled in the past by Denmark. The plain square-ended flag is the civil flag. Cut into a swallow-tail shape it becomes the naval ensign and state flag.

# DJIBOUTI

*East Africa*

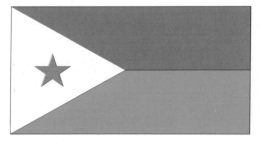

**Republic of Djibouti**
**Flag ratio 1:2**
Djibouti (formerly French Somaliland) won
independence from France in 1977, and its new flag
was based on that of the Ligue Populaire pour
l'Indépendence (People's League for Independence),
leaders in the independence struggle. The party had
used the same basic flag since 1972: two horizontal
bands of blue over green represent the people – blue
for the Issas, who are Somalis (Somalia has a light
blue flag) and green for the Afars, who are Muslims
(green being a colour traditionally used to represent
Islam). The white triangle in the hoist symbolises
equality and peace, while the five-pointed red star
centred in the triangle stands for national unity.

*Caribbean*

# DOMINICA

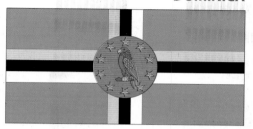

**Commonwealth of Dominica**

**Flag ratio 1:2**

The sisserou parrot, central feature of Dominica's flag, is the unique national bird; it stands for high national aspirations. It is surrounded by 10 green stars, for the island's parishes. They are set in a red roundel to show commitment to social justice. The roundel appears on a cross of yellow, black and white, the three strands representing the Holy Trinity and the colours symbolising: sunshine, agriculture and the native people (yellow); the purity of the people's aspirations, and of local water (white); the soil and the people's African heritage (black). The green field is for the island vegetation. The flag echoes Dominica's motto, *Après Bondie C'est La Ter* ('After the Good Lord Comes the Land').

# DOMINICAN REPUBLIC    *Caribbean*

**Dominican Republic**

**Flag ratio 2:3**

The Dominican Republic lies in the east of Hispaniola, the island it shares with Haiti, its former invader. The flag shows the struggle against Haiti, with the white cross of liberty superimposed on the blue and red of Haiti's flag (the blue and red in the fly were later transposed). The flag was adopted on independence in 1844. Red now symbolises the freedom fighters' suffering, blue liberty and the white cross the people's sacrifices. The state flag has the national arms in the centre: a shield of the state colours with a gold cross and open Bible. Around are palm and laurel branches and a scroll bears the freedom fighters' motto: *Dios, Patria, Libertad* ('God, Country, Liberty').

*Eastern Asia*

# EAST TIMOR

**Democratic Republic of Timor–Leste**
**Flag ratio 1:2**
As the name suggest, East Timor is the eastern part
of the island of Timor. The western part belongs to
Indonesia. While Indonesia was colonised by the
Netherlands, East Timor was a Portuguese possession
until 1975. In December 1975, East Timor declared
independence and a flag similar to the present one
was hoisted. Indonesian forces annexed the country on
17 July 1976. In 1999, the UN took over administration
of the territory and it became fully independent on
20 May 2002. The flag is based on that of Fretilin, the
leading political party. Red is for the blood of those
who died for freedom, black is the sad past and gold
the bright future. The star, which has one point
towards the hoist, is for freedom.

# ECUADOR

*South America*

**Republic of Ecuador**
**Flag ratio 1:2**
As with Colombia and Venezuela, the flag of Ecuador is
based on that of the South American liberators Simón
Bolívar and Francisco de Miranda. The three countries
originally federated as Gran Colombia, but this soon
dissolved. Yellow is for golden America, blue for the sea
and red for Imperial Spain. The arms show Chimborazo,
Ecuador's highest peak, with emblems for trade below.
Four zodiac signs show the period in 1845 when
Ecuador fought for independence, symbolised by
the sun. A condor above represents freedom and
the fasces (a bundle of rods containing an axe) below
the authority of the republic. The arms are surrounded
by a trophy of flags and weapons. Without the arms
the plain tricolour is the civil flag and civil ensign.

*North Africa*      **EGYPT**

**Arab Republic of Egypt**
**Flag ratio 2:3**

Like many of its neighbours, Egypt uses the colours
of the Pan-Arab movement. The flag has been through
several changes. The monarchy was overthrown in
1952 and a republic declared. In 1958, Egypt and
Syria formed the United Arab Republic, using a flag
like Syria's present design. The union broke up in
1961. From 1972 until 1977, Egypt, Syria and Libya
formed the Federation of Arab Republics. The national
arms replaced the previous two stars. The present
form of the arms is the eagle of Saladin (12th-century
sultan and opponent of the Crusaders), bearing on its
breast a shield in the national colours. On the flag the
emblem is entirely in gold.

# EL SALVADOR

*Central America*

**Republic of El Salvador**
**Flag ratio 3:5**
El Salvador's flag, adopted in 1912, is similar to the flags of the members of the United Provinces of Central America (see Costa Rica). There are three versions: plain for the civil flag; with the motto *Dios, Union, Libertad* ('God, Unity, Liberty') in the white band for the merchant flag; and with the arms in the white band for the state flag and ensign (main image). These show a triangle, for equality, and contain a scene of five mountains (the federation members) between two seas, with a cap of liberty above and a shining sun. Around is the date of liberation from Spain (15 September 1821) and a rainbow under the triangle's apex. The national colours and motto also feature.

*Western Europe* **ENGLAND**

**England**

**Flag ratio 3:5**

The accepted, though unofficial, national flag of England is the Cross of St George. This flag dates from the Third Crusade, the first time that kings led national contingents on Crusade. To distinguish them, different coloured crosses were to be worn by different nationalities. After some confusion, the red cross on white was accepted by the English. It was only later that this was described as the 'Cross of St George', after the patron saint of England. This is still the accepted national flag of England, and is seen especially on sporting occasions when England is represented separately. When the first Union Flag was designed in 1606, the St George Cross was placed on the St Andrew flag of Scotland.

# EQUATORIAL GUINEA     *West Africa*

**Republic of Equatorial Guinea**
**Flag ratio 5:8**
A former Spanish colony which gained independence in 1968, Equatorial Guinea's flags reflect the country's ideals and characteristics. The flag, also adopted in 1968, is a tricolour with horizontal bands of green, white and red to symbolise agriculture, peace and independence respectively. The blue triangle in the hoist is for the sea, which both divides the mainland from and links it to the country's five offshore islands. The arms in the white band bears a shield with an indigenous silk cotton tree topped by six gold stars, for the main-land and five islands. A scroll below has the national motto: *Unidad, Paz, Justicia* ('Unity, Peace, Justice').

*East Africa*

# ERITREA

**Eritrea**
**Flag ratio 2:3**

Eritrea gained its freedom in May 1993 after the collapse of the Communist regime in Ethiopia. It had been an autonomous province of Ethiopia, with its own flag, until 1959, and the old flag, together with the flag of the Eritrean People's Liberation Front, has been used as the basis for the new. The olive wreath and stem are features from the old flag, themselves originally inspired by the flag of the United Nations. The rest of the flag is derived from the Eritrean People's Liberation Front flag, with the olive wreath replacing the yellow star previously appearing in the red triangle.

# ESTONIA

*Eastern Europe*

**Republic of Estonia**
**Flag ratio 7:11**

The tricolour of Estonia was first used in risings against occupying Russian forces in 1881. The Russians frowned on use of the flag, but after the break-up of their empire in 1917 Estonia enjoyed a period of freedom during which its blue, black and white tricolour again became the national flag. It was suppressed again after invasion by Stalinist forces in 1940 but became the national flag once more in 1990, as the USSR disintegrated. The blue stands for the sky and the mutual fidelity of the people; black for the soil and the Estonians' mythological ancestors; and white for the peoples' wish for freedom, and for the snow which covers this Baltic country for six months each year.

*East Africa*                    # ETHIOPIA

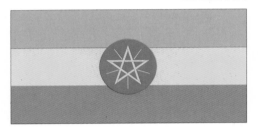

**Federal Democratic Republic of Ethiopia**
**Flag ratio 1:2**
The Ethiopian flag is one of the most influential in
the world. It is the basis for the Pan-African colours
of green, yellow and red. This is because Ethiopia is
the oldest independent African country. The colours
were first used in the 1890s, as three pennants in no
special order. The order was settled and they became
a modern flag early in the 20th century. The colours
are symbolic in Coptic Christianity, representing the
Holy Trinity and the virtues of Faith, Hope and
Charity. In 1996, the new national emblem was added
to the tricolour to create a new all-purpose flag for
government and civil use.

# FALKLAND ISLANDS    *S Atlantic Ocean*

**Colony of the Falkland Islands**
**Flag ratio 1:2**
Together with South Georgia and the South Sandwich Islands, the Falkland Islands are a British territory. They were discovered in 1592, since when several countries, including France, Spain and Argentina, have claimed them. The flag is a British Blue Ensign, with the badge in the fly. The shield depicts a sheep standing on an island, representing the wool industry. On the sea is a ship, the *Desire*. Below is the motto 'Desire the Right'. The *Desire* was the English ship which discovered the Falklands, and the motto refers to it and to Britain's claim to the islands.

*Scandinavia
(N Atlantic Ocean)*

# FAROE ISLANDS

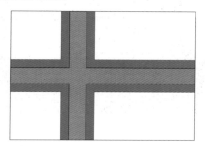

**Faroe Islands**
**Flag ratio 8:11**

First settled by Norse people in the 9th century, then passing to Danish control in 1380 after the union of the Norwegian and Danish crowns, the Faroes have been under Scandinavian influence for centuries, and this is evident in the design of their flag. Although the islands are still a part of the Kingdom of Denmark (see corner flag), they have had an autonomous legislature since the mid-1940s, with the flag first being adopted in 1948. The colours of Denmark are reversed out to an off-centre red cross on a white field. The cross is fimbriated in blue, possibly a reference to past Norwegian influences.

# FIJI

*Pacific Ocean*

**Republic of the Fiji Islands**
**Flag ratio 1:2**
Ties with Britain are stressed in the flag of Fiji,
a former colony. The design dates from 1970, when
the islands gained their independence, and is based
on the Blue Ensign, although with a paler blue in the
field. The continuing connection with the United
Kingdom is displayed in the Union Jack in the canton,
while a modified version of Fiji's state arms is in the fly.
The chief, at the top of the shield, displays an English
lion holding a cocoa pod. Below this the shield is
quartered by the cross of St George with, in the four
corners, a sugar cane plant, a coconut palm, a bunch
of bananas (all these being indigenous plants) and
a white dove of peace bearing an olive branch.

*Scandinavia* # FINLAND

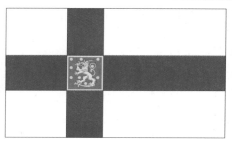

**Republic of Finland**
**Flag ratio 11:18**
The identification of Finland with the Norse nations is reflected clearly in its flag. Finland was conquered by Sweden in the 12th century, but passed into Russian control in 1809. The chance for independence was seized when Russia was in revolution in 1917, and although the flag was adopted then, its design dated from the 19th century. The blue and white represent the Finnish lakes and snow. The state flag (main image) has the national arms in the centre of the cross: a red field containing a lion rampant with a mailed arm bearing a sword, and treading on a scimitar, representing national resistance to eastern invaders, Its design dates from the 16th century.

# FRANCE

*Western Europe*

**French Republic**
**Flag ratio 2:3**

The colours, design and underlying philosophy of the French Republic's flag have made it the most influential in the world. Since its adoption in 1794, the tricolour design or its colours or both, have been used by revolutionary movements and new nations the world over to represent their ideals and their spirit. The colours are thought to be the blue and red of Paris, and white for the Bourbon monarchy, although they have other associations dating back to the reign of Charlemagne (c.742–814). The austere 1794 design, a deliberately radical departure from the more fussy flags of the time, symbolised the new republican principles.

*Pacific Ocean*

# FRENCH POLYNESIA

**Territory of French Polynesia**
**Flag ratio 2:3**
This island group in the South Pacific gained home rule from France in 1984, and the flag was adopted then. Red and white had historically been used in flags in the area, and particularly on one of the islands, Tahiti, since the early 19th century. The central emblem depicts a pirogue, a type of canoe, on the sea over which a sun is shining. The figures on the pirogue represent Gambier, Marquesas, Society, Tuamotu and Tubai, the five island groups. As a territory of France (see corner flag), the islands' flag is flown only in conjunction with the French tricolour.

# FRIESIAN ISLANDS     *Scandinavia (N Sea)*

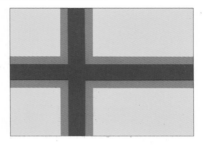

**Friesian Islands**
**Flag ratio 8:11**
Although the Friesian Islands actually belong to
Germany (see corner flag), the Scandinavian origin of
most of the islands' inhabitants is reflected in the use
of the distinctive off-centre Scandinavian cross in the
flag. The flag's colours are taken from the arms of the
islands.

*Central Africa* **GABON**

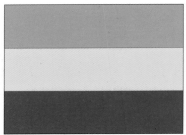

**Republic of Gabon**
**Flag ratio 3:4**
Once a part of France's African empire, Gabon gained
its independence in 1960. However, the influence of
the French tricolour can be seen in the design of its
flag, which is a horizontal tricolour of green, yellow
and blue, a combination of the French and Pan-
African colours of African unity. The green represents
the country's rainforests and the lumber industry,
the source of much of the nation's wealth; the yellow
represents the sun; and the blue stands for the sea.
A former design, dropped just before independence,
had a narrower yellow band and a French tricolour
in the canton.

# GAMBIA

*West Africa*

**Republic of The Gambia**
**Flag ratio 2:3**
The Gambia, the smallest African country, was a colony of Britain from 1843 until it gained its independence in 1965. The new national flag was adopted at this time. It has three broad bands of red, blue and green, separated by two fimbriations of white. The green is symbolic of the land, while the blue represents the Gambia River flowing over it, and the red stands for the hot sun beating down on both.

*Eastern Europe*  **GEORGIA**

**Republic of Georgia**
**Flag ratio 2:3**

Shortly before achieving independence from the
USSR, Georgia readopted the flag it had used during
its brief period of freedom 1918–20. In January 2004
this flag was replaced by a design which was even
older, and which had also appeared in 1990. The flag
is based on one used by Queen Tamar, a queen of
Georgia in the 13th century. The white field and red
cross are the flag of St George, seen also in other
countries. The four small crosses have been variously
described as of Roman or Orthodox origin.

# GERMANY

*Western Europe*

**Federal Republic of Germany**

**Flag ratio 3:5**

Black and gold were the colours of the first German Empire. German troops fighting against Napoleon in 1813 wore black uniforms with red facings and gold buttons. These colours were used as a flag by those wanting to unify the German states. This flag was first adopted in 1848, but never officially accepted. When German unity was established in 1871, the first flag of the united country was a black–white–red horizontal tricolour. The German Republic of 1919 adopted the black–red–gold, but it was abolished by the Nazi regime in 1933. When German independence was restored in 1949, this flag was also restored. The state flag has the arms of a black eagle on a gold shield in the centre.

*West Africa*                                    # GHANA

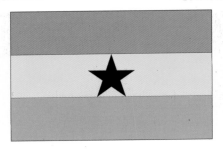

**Republic of Ghana**
**Flag ratio 2:3**
Ghana was the first of the liberated African nations
to take as its colours those of Ethiopia and the Pan-
African movement of African unity. The colours of this
flag, however, are also symbolic in themselves: red is
taken to represent the blood of the freedom fighters
who died for independence, yellow is the mineral
wealth of the country (when a British colony, Ghana
was known as the Gold Coast), and green is the rich
forests. The black, five-pointed star set in the centre
of the yellow band represents the lodestar of African
freedom. The Ghanaian flag was seminal in its
influence on the subsequent adoption of flags by
former African colonies throughout the 1960s.

# GIBRALTAR

*Western Europe*

**Colony of Gibraltar**
**Flag ratio 1:2**
Gibraltar was one of the ancient Pillars of Hercules
which delimited the known world to Europeans.
It was ceded to Britain by Spain in 1713 and is a self-
governing colony, so its official flag is the Blue Ensign.
It features in the fly the city arms given to Gibraltar
by Ferdinand and Isabella of Spain in 1502 and shows
a key hanging from a three-turreted castle, both
symbols of Gibraltar's strategic importance as gateway
to the Mediterranean. Below is a scroll with the motto
*Montis Insignia Calpe* ('Emblem of Mount Calpe' – the
rock's original name). The city flag, with the arms set
on two unequal bands of white over red, is popular
with Gibraltarians and has been used since 1966.

*Eastern Europe*                                    **GREECE**

**Hellenic Republic**
**Flag ratio 7:12**

The blue and white colours of the Greek flag were
first used in the 1820s and 1830s during the
country's war of independence against the Turkish
Ottoman Empire. The nine blue and white stripes
are said to represent the nine syllables of the national
motto, *Eleutheria a Thanatos* ('Liberty or Death'), the
Greek battle cry in the war. The white cross in the
canton represents Orthodox Christianity. The flag
was adopted in its present form in 1978. It was used
previously, often with another flag, plain blue with
a white cross, now seen only in an unofficial capacity
within the country.

# GREENLAND

*Arctic Ocean*

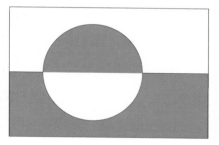

**Greenland**

**Flag ratio 5:9**

The world's largest island, Greenland was settled by native American hunters some 3,000 years before Europeans arrived in about AD 982. Norwegians settled the island in the 10th century, but the island passed to Denmark, when the Danish and Norwegian crowns united. From the 18th century, Greenland was run by the Royal Greenland Trading Company. In the 1950s it became part of Denmark (see corner flag), and has been self-governing since 1979. Its flag was the winner in a competition and was adopted in 1985. The red and white of Denmark remain, but now show a far-northern scene, with white representing inland ice and icebergs and the red the sunrise and sunset.

*Caribbean* **GRENADA**

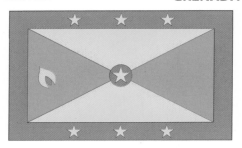

State of Grenada

Flag ratio 2:3

The flag of Grenada was adopted in 1974 on independence from Britain. It is quartered by two diagonals, with two yellow triangles top and bottom, and two green triangles in the hoist and fly. A red border surrounds these, with six five-pointed yellow stars along top and bottom, and a seventh in a red disc in the centre of the diagonals. The seven stars represent the island's parishes, and the nutmeg in the green triangle of the hoist shows the island's main resource. The colours, too, are symbolic: green is for agriculture and the land; yellow the sunshine; and red freedom and the people's fervour. They are also the colours of the nationalist Pan-African movement.

# GUAM

*Pacific Ocean*

**Guam**
**Flag ratio 21:40**
A strategically important island in the Western
Pacific, Guam is a dependency of the United States
of America (see corner flag). It was taken by the US
from Spain in 1898 and is now home to an American
naval and air base. Guam has had a measure of self-
government since 1950. Its flag was adopted in 1917,
and comprises a red-bordered blue field with a red-
bordered oval in the centre, showing a beach with
a palm tree and small sailing craft, with the island's
name in red capitals. The flag of Guam is flown only
in conjunction with that of the US.

*Central America*

# GUATEMALA

**Republic of Guatemala**

**Flag ratio 2:3**

Guatemala was a member of the United Provinces of Central America, who broke away from Spanish rule in 1821 (see Costa Rica for details). The federation broke up 18 years later but all five nations retained the same basic flag. Guatemala changed its bands from a horizontal to a vertical design in 1871. The state flag (main image) has the national arms in the centre but unlike other members' they are not based on the federation arms. They feature a quetzal bird on a scroll bearing the date of independence, 15 September 1821. Set behind are arms, showing readiness to defend the country, and a laurel wreath. Guatemala's arms were adopted in 1825 and reached their present appearance in 1968.

# GUERNSEY *Western Europe (English Channel)*

**Guernsey**
**Flag ratio 2:3**

Guernsey, like Jersey, is one of the Channel Isles. For a long time it flew the plain flag of St George. In 1985 a different flag was adopted. This kept the St George Cross, but added a golden cross with splayed ends to it. The origin of the gold cross is in the Bayeux Tapestry. This is an embroidery showing the conquest of England by Duke William of Normandy. His flag, shown on the tapestry, has as its central emblem a gold cross of this type. So the flag of Guernsey strongly recalls its Norman history. At sea, vessels registered in Guernsey use the usual British Red Ensign, with the gold cross added in the fly, but only between the islands and the British mainland.

# GUINEA

**Republic of Guinea**
**Flag ratio 2:3**

The Pan-African movement's colours and the French tricolour's design and proportions were the inspirations for Guinea's flag of red, yellow and green vertical bands. Guinea gained independence from France in 1958 and, following Ghana's lead of the previous year, adopted the green, yellow and red expressive of African solidarity and a desire for unity. In Guinea's case, the colours also reflect the three words of the national motto, *Travail, Justice, Solidarité*; work is represented by red, justice by yellow and solidarity by green. They were also the colours of the Partie Démocratique du Guinea, then the dominant political party, which had led the country to independence.

# GUINEA-BISSAU

*West Africa*

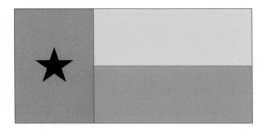

**Republic of Guinea-Bissau**
**Flag ratio 1:2**

Guinea-Bissau's flag was adopted in 1973 when the country became independent from Portugal. The flag is based on one used by the liberation movement since the early 1960s, which in turn was probably based on the flag of Ghana, first of the former African colonies to achieve independence. The red, yellow and green are the colours of the Pan-African movement, and the black star is also expressive of a desire for African unity. But in the flag of Guinea-Bissau the colours are also symbolic in their own right: red for the blood of the fallen heroes of the independence movement; green for hope; yellow for the sun, source of life; and the black star for the African continent.

*South America* # GUYANA

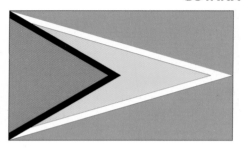

**Co-operative Republic of Guyana**
**Flag ratio 3:5**
The flag of this former British colony was designed to reflect the country's physical attributes and the qualities of its people. The flag has two triangles pointing out from the hoist – a smaller red one and a larger gold one spanning the fly, fimbriated in black and white respectively – on a green field. The red is said to represent the energy of the people in building the new country, while the gold symbolises the mineral wealth and the country's forward thrust, maintained by perseverance (black). The white fimbriation symbolises the rivers, and the green field its agriculture and forests. The flag was adopted in 1966, the same year Guyana achieved its independence.

# HAITI

*Caribbean*

**Republic of Haiti**
**Flag ratio 3:5**

Two national flags have been used in turn since Haiti became independent in 1804. The first, of two bands, blue over red, was readopted most recently in 1986 when the Duvalier regime fell. Supposedly modelled on the French flag, it was used from around 1804 and its colours stand for the country's two communities, the blacks (blue) and mulattoes (red). The state flag has the national arms in a white central panel: a palm tree topped by a cap of liberty and surrounded by weapons, with the motto *L'union fait la force* ('Unity gives strength'). The rival flag, of vertical black and red bands, was used in the early 1800s and readopted in 1964 by the discredited Duvalier government.

*Central America*

# HONDURAS

**Republic of Honduras**
**Flag ratio 1:2**
Like Costa Rica, a member of the United Provinces of
Central America, Honduras' flag was officially adopted
in 1866. Five stars show hope for reunification of the
provinces. The naval ensign has arms. The arms are
a triangle for equality and justice, on a shore behind
two towers for independence. These are set in an
oval border which is inscribed in Spanish 'Free,
Sovereign, Independent', with the date of independence,
15 September 1821. Above are arrows for the original
inhabitants, cornucopias for prosperity, with trees and
industrial emblems completing the design. The arms do
not appear on the state flag, only on the naval ensign.

# HONG KONG

*Eastern Asia*

**Hong Kong**
**Flag ratio 2:3**

When Hong Kong was a British possession, it used a British Blue Ensign with the colony's badge, dating from 1959, in the fly. In July 1997 the territory reverted to China (see corner flag), but remained a Special Administrative Region with its own flag. The new flag, like the Chinese flag, is red to represent Communism and features a central emblem of a bauhinia, a local flower which has also appeared on Hong Kong stamps since 1968. The five red stars within the petals also recall the flag of China.

*Eastern Europe*  # HUNGARY

**Republic of Hungary**
**Flag ratio 2:3**
The colours of this flag have their origins in the 9th century when Árpad, leader of the Magyars (then rulers of Hungary), adopted a plain red flag as his own. After the country's conversion in the 10th century, a cross on a white field was used, but by the 15th century red, white and green together were the national colours. Their arrangement in a horizontal tricolour dates from 1848, a year of revolutions in Europe, to inspire those seeking independence from empire. After Communism fell in 1989–90, the original national arms were restored and, with the tricolour, they form the state flag. They show the arms of Árpad and traditional crown of St Stephen, first Christian king of Hungary.

# ICELAND

*Scandinavia (N Atlantic)*

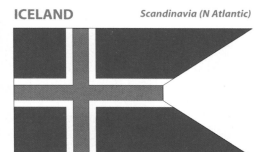

**Republic of Iceland**
**Flag ratio 5:7**

Invaded and colonised by Vikings from Norway in the 9th century, Iceland has the distinction of having held Europe's first parliament in 930. The country was ruled by Norway in the 13th and 14th centuries but when the Norwegians lost their independence to Denmark, Iceland passed to the Danes, too. The current flag was adopted in 1918 when Iceland became a separate realm in the Kingdom of Denmark, and became the national flag on independence in 1944. It is the same as the Norwegian flag – itself modelled on the Danish – with the blue and red colours reversed. The Scandinavian cross and Norwegian colours show Icelandic affiliations lie with the Norse countries.

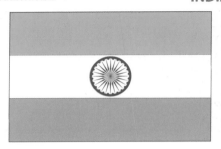

*Southern Asia*                    **INDIA**

**Republic of India**
**Flag ratio 2:3**
The flag of the nationalist Indian National Congress
party was used as the basis for the national flag in 1947.
The layout was influenced by the French tricolour,
and the colours are symbolic: saffron is for courage
and sacrifice; white truth and peace; and green faith
and chivalry. The Congress flag's spinning wheel
motif was replaced by the blue chakra, or Buddhist
wheel. The chakra comes from the Indian national
arms depicting four lions, one facing each direction,
standing on a pedestal into which four wheels are set.
The arms come from the capital, or upper part, of a
column erected by the first Buddhist emperor, Asoka,
in the holy city of Sarnath in the 3rd century BC.

# INDONESIA

*Eastern Asia*

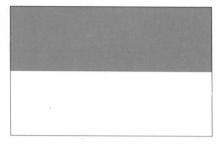

**Republic of Indonesia**
**Flag ratio 2:3**
The Majapahit Empire in 13th-century Indonesia had a red and white flag as its banner, and these colours – considered holy colours at that time – were used in the region down the centuries. Their 20th-century revival was as an expression of nationalism against the Dutch who had controlled Indonesia through the Dutch East India Company since the 18th century. The current flag was first used this century in the 1920s, being adopted officially as the national flag of the republic in 1945 when the country declared its independence. Its red over white bands stand for courage, and justice and purity respectively. Except for its proportions, it is identical to the flag of Monaco.

*Middle East*

# IRAN

Islamic Republic of Iran

**Flag ratio 4:7**

The Iranian flag colours are traditional, probably dating from the 18th century, and can be taken to represent Islam (green), peace (white) and courage (red). They were formed into a tricolour in 1907. The traditional centrepiece of a lion with a sword standing before a rising sun, with a crown above, was abolished after the shah abdicated in 1979. The new centrepiece combines elements representing Islam which, taken together in this device, represent Allah (God). The white markings repeat Allah-o-Akbar ('God is Great') 22 times. This number represents the date in the Jallali Muslim calendar when the Islamic Revolution toppled the shah's rule.

# IRAQ

*Middle East*

**Republic of Iraq**
**Flag ratio 2:3**

The Pan-Arab colours of black, green, white and red
were adopted by Arab nationalists in the early
20th century as they fought the Turks. Traditionally
the colours are said to represent the qualities of
Muslims: courage (red), generosity (white), the triumphs
of Islam (black) and the religion (green). The flag's
pattern dates from 1963, when the royal regime
established after World War I was overthrown. It was
based on the Egyptian flag of the time, with the same
pattern of bands. The three stars in the centre band
represent the then-hoped-for unity of Iraq, Syria and
Egypt. The slogan Allah-o-Akbar ('God is Great') was
added during the 1991 Gulf War.

*Western Europe*

# IRELAND

**Republic of Ireland**
**Flag ratio 1:2**
The Irish tricolour was based on the French flag
and was first used by the nationalist Young Ireland
movement in 1848 in their struggle for freedom
from Britain. The green is for the Catholic, Gaelic
and Anglo-Norman communities, orange is for the
planter northern Protestants and white in the centre
signifies a hope of peace and trust between them.
It was chosen as the national flag in 1920 over the
older Green Flag (of a gold harp, supposedly of King
Brian Boru, on an emerald field) favoured since the
19th century by the Home Rule movement. The Green
Flag today is the jack of the Irish Navy, while the
president's flag carries the same motif on a blue field.

# ISLE OF MAN

*Western Europe (Irish Sea)*

**Isle of Man**
**Flag ratio 1:2**
The Isle of Man has a curious design on its flag. The red field has three legs, joined at the hip and encased in armour, forming a kind of wheel. This is an ancient emblem of the island which has been used on flags and other emblems for several hundred years. It is often shown in other patterns, even reversed, but the style shown here is official. Like Guernsey, the civil ensign of the Isle of Man is a British Red Ensign, with the emblem added in the fly. Again, this may only be used in coastal waters and between the isle and the British mainland.

*Middle East*          # ISRAEL

**State of Israel**
**Flag ratio 8:11**
The distinctive flag of Israel bears in its centre the
Magen David, or Shield of David, a Jewish emblem for
over 700 years. The pattern of white and blue bands
derives from the pattern on the tallith, the Jewish prayer
shawl. The design emerged in the late 19th century
and had its origins in the Zionist movement, the
nationalist movement which sought to reestablish a
Jewish homeland in Palestine. It was officially adopted
as the national flag on the establishment of the State
of Israel in 1948. The ensigns also feature the star, while
the flag of the president features the official emblem of
the state, the menorah, the seven-branched candlestick
which is an ancient symbol of the Jewish people.

# ITALY

*Western Europe*

**Italian Republic**
**Flag ratio 2:3**
Based on the French flag, the Italian tricolour was
first used in 1796 in northern Italy, when a French
occupation released the area from Austrian rule. The
tricolour became a popular Italian nationalist banner
in the wars of unification which lasted through much
of the 19th century. In 1861, the Italian states were
united under King Victor Emmanuel II of Savoy.
Rome became the capital after it was annexed in 1870.
The green–white–red tricolour became the national
flag, with the arms of Savoy in the centre. When Italy
became a republic in 1946, the royal arms were
removed from the flag.

*Caribbean*

# JAMAICA

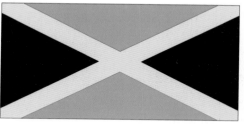

Jamaica

**Flag ratio 1:2**

A saltire forms the main feature of the flag of
Jamaica, but it is used purely as a design feature
and does not represent any martyr or saint. The gold
saltire divides the flag into four triangles: two green,
at the top and bottom, and two black, at the hoist
and fly. The colours used represent the island's
natural resources and the sun (gold), its agricultural
wealth and hope (green), and the hardships which
have been overcome and which are to be faced
(black). Together, the colours symbolise the motto
'Hardships there are but the land is green and the
sun shineth'. The flag was officially adopted in 1962
when Jamaica became independent from Britain.

# JAPAN

*Eastern Asia (Pacific Ocean)*

Japan
**Flag ratio 2:3**
Japan's flag refers to its being known as the 'Land of the Rising Sun', the most easterly country in Asia. Legend says that the Japanese are descended from the Sun goddess Amaterasu. Certainly the sun emblem has been used by the Japanese emperors for over 1,000 years. The national flag is the 'Hino Maru' (Lucky Sun), a plain white field with a red disk. Although of ancient use, it was only adopted officially in 1870, when Japan first sent diplomatic delegations to other countries. The Japanese naval ensign is also white with the sun, but set towards the hoist and emitting 16 red rays.

*Western Europe (English Channel)*  **JERSEY**

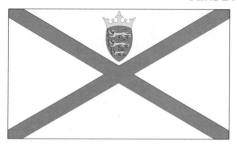

Jersey
**Flag ratio 2:3**
The flag of the island of Jersey is the result of a
mistake. On a Dutch flag chart, a white flag with a red
saltire appeared, marked 'Ierse Vlag'. Someone read
this as 'Jersey Flag', but it meant 'Irish Flag'. Since then
it has been accepted as the flag of the island. For a
long time the flag was the plain red saltire on white.
More recently a shield has been added with the
ancient arms of the Duchy of Normandy. The Channel
Isles were part of Normandy, and are the only part
which remain under United Kingdom rule.

# JORDAN

*Middle East*

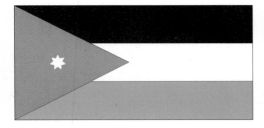

**Hashemite Kingdom of Jordan**
**Flag ratio 1:2**

As part of the Turkish Ottoman Empire at the beginning of the 20th century, Jordan was one of several aspirant nations to adopt the black, red, white and green of Pan-Arab nationalism. The original flag, used in the World War I Arab revolt against the Turks, had the colours black over green over white, but the present order was established in 1921, and the star was added in 1928. Its seven points represent the first seven verses of the Koran, the Holy Book of Islam. The star also distinguishes the Jordanian flag from that of Palestine.

*Western Asia*

# KAZAKHSTAN

**Republic of Kazakhstan**
**Flag ratio 1:2**
The new flag of Kazakhstan was adopted in June 1992, the year after the break-up of the USSR, of which Kazakhstan had been a member. On the sky-blue field are a golden sun and a soaring eagle, and in the hoist is a vertical stripe described as the 'national ornamentation'. The blue field represents the sky, and the sun and the eagle stand for the lofty aspirations of the Kazak people. The blue is of a similar colour to that used in the country's old SSR flag. The eagle itself is of a species known locally as the *berkut*, or Steppe eagle.

# KENYA

*East Africa*

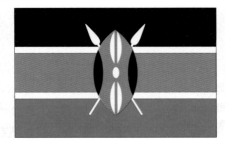

**Republic of Kenya**
**Flag ratio 5:9**
Kenya was a British colony until independence in 1963.
Its flag was adopted that year and comprises three
horizontal bands of black, red and green, separated
by two narrow white bands. The colours are said to
represent the African people, the blood common to
all humanity, and the fertility of the land of Kenya.
The Masai shield and crossed spears in the centre
represent the defence of national freedom. The colours
are also those of the Kenya African National Union
Party which led the independence movement and
formed the government until 1992. The white is for
peace and national unity, the colour being from the
flag of the rival Kenya African Democratic Union Party.

*Pacific Ocean*

# KIRIBATI

**Republic of Kiribati**

**Flag ratio 3:5**

Formerly known as the Gilbert Islands, Kiribati, together with the Ellice Islands (now Tuvalu), was a British protectorate from 1892 and a colony from 1916. The process of separation of the two island groups began in 1975, and Kiribati (the local pronunciation of the word 'Gilberts') achieved independence in 1979. The flag was adopted in the same year and has blue and white wavy bands, representing the Pacific Ocean, over which a sun is rising in a red sky. A local yellow frigate bird flies over the scene. The flag was based on the arms of the former colony.

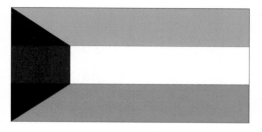

# KUWAIT

*Middle East*

**State of Kuwait**

**Flag ratio 1:2**

The Pan-Arab colours feature on Kuwait's flag. Once part of the Turkish Ottoman Empire, Kuwait was a British protectorate from 1899 until 1961. In that year the country gained independence and the flag was adopted. It is a horizontal tricolour of green, white and red, with a black trapezium at the hoist. A similar shape appeared on the 1932–58 flag of Iraq. According to a well-known Arabic poem, green is for fertility, white for glorious deeds, red for chivalry and military skill, and black for the battlefields where the enemies suffered defeat.

*Western Asia*

# KYRGYZSTAN

**Kyrgyzstan**

**Flag ratio 3:5**

In 1992, the year after the break-up of the USSR, the new flag of this former Soviet Socialist Republic came into being. It comprises a 40-rayed sun centred in a field of red. The sun's rays stand for the 40 tribes which merged to become the Kyrgyz nation, and the national hero, Manas the Noble, is represented by the red field. Within the sun is depicted a bird's-eye view of a yurt, the traditional tent used by the nomadic people of the Steppes. The roof, or *tunduk*, of the yurt represents the traditional heart and home of these nomadic tribes.

# LAOS

*Eastern Asia*

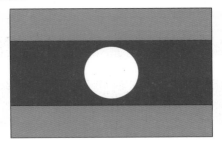

**Lao People's Democratic Republic**
**Flag ratio 2:3**
This is one of the few Communist flags not to use a five-pointed star emblem. Adopted when the country became a republic in 1975, it has a white disc in its centre symbolising the people's unity under the Lao People's Revolutionary Party. The red stands for the blood shed by the people in defence of their country, and blue symbolises the nation's wealth. The flag belonged to the Pathet Lao, or Lao Patriotic Front, who battled with royalist government forces after independence from France. This flag replaced the royalist flag of three elephants standing under a parasol on five steps, representing in its various elements the monarchy, the people and their Buddhist faith.

# LATVIA

**Republic of Latvia**

**Flag ratio 1:2**

Conflicting stories exist to explain the tribar of Latvia. It was first mentioned in a chronicle of 1280, when a force from a northern region carried it as the banner of their castle. Another legend tells of a Latvian tribal leader, wounded in battle and laid on a white sheet. Where he lay the sheet stayed white but the sides folded over him were stained by his blood. The banner was described as 'red with a white cut'. This vague description was interpreted as the present flag in 1918. Latvia was invaded several times through history, and was under Russian rule between 1789 and 1918. The flag had been used secretly under Russian rule and was adopted officially at independence. In 1940 Latvia lost its independence to the USSR. When it was regained in 1991 the traditional flag was revived.

# LEBANON

*Middle East*

**Republic of Lebanon**
**Flag ratio 2:3**
The symbol of a cedar tree, an ancient symbol of Lebanon since biblical times, is the centrepiece of the flag of the Lebanese Republic. Following World War I and the break-up of the Ottoman Empire, Lebanon was administered by France, and the cedar appeared on the white band of the French tricolour. The present flag was adopted on independence in 1943. The red and white bands are thought to have been the colours of the Lebanese Legion in World War I, and officially they represent respectively the sacrifices of the people for independence, and purity, while the cedar tree symbolises happiness and prosperity for the country.

*Southern Africa*

# LESOTHO

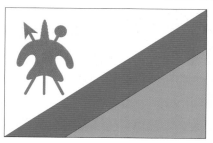

**Kingdom of Lesotho**

**Flag ratio 2:3**

Lesotho has had two flags since independence in 1966. The first had narrow green and red vertical bands at the hoist and a blue field with a white straw hat, symbol of the country's Basotho people, in its centre. But the colours were those of the main Lesotho National Party, and a new flag was adopted after a coup in 1986. The present flag is divided diagonally from the top of the fly to the base of the hoist: the white upper half represents peace, and bears a shield with two crossed weapons at the hoist, showing the Basotho people's means of maintaining peace and independence. The broad blue band in the lower half stands for rain, while the green triangle symbolises prosperity.

# LIBERIA

*West Africa*

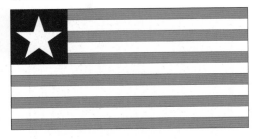

**Republic of Liberia**
**Flag ratio 10:19**
Liberia was settled in 1822 by the American
Colonisation Society as a homeland for freed American
slaves. A similar form of flag to that ultimately
adopted was in use at that time but was modified to
its present form on independence in 1847. Its design
is clearly based on the American Stars and Stripes.
There are 11 red and white stripes in the field, to
represent the 11 men who signed Liberia's declaration
of independence. The blue of the canton stands for
Africa, while the five-pointed white star refers to
Liberia's status at the time of its gaining independence
as the only independent African nation.

**Socialist People's Libyan Arab Jamahiriya**
**Flag ratio 2:3**

Prior to 1977, the Libyan national flag comprised the Pan-Arab colours of red, white and black in a design identical to that of Egypt, with whom Libya was in federation at that time. But in 1977 Egypt made peace with its traditional enemy, Israel, in a move that angered many Arab nations. In a reaction to this Israeli–Egyptian pact, Libya adopted its current flag, the plain green field symbolising its Green Revolution (which emphasised agriculture and the need for self-sufficiency in food) and the nation's continuing adherence to Islam. Two years later, in 1979, Libya also left the Federation of Arab Republics, which it had co-founded with Egypt and Syria.

# LIECHTENSTEIN

*Western Europe*

**Principality of Liechtenstein**
**Flag ratio 3:5**
The principality of Liechtenstein was created in 1719 following the union of the countships of Vaduz and Schellenberg. The blue and red of the flag have been used as the national colours since the early 19th century, and the gold crown was added to the canton in 1937 to avoid any confusion with the flag of Haiti. When this flag is flown vertically, the crown appears rotated through 90° so that its cross continues to point towards the top of the flag. The state flag is also a bicolour of blue over red, but with the arms of Liechtenstein in the centre and without the crown in the canton.

*Eastern Europe*

# LITHUANIA

**Republic of Lithuania**

**Flag ratio 2:3**

Lithuania's yellow, green and red tricolour was first adopted as the national flag in 1918, with official sanction following four years later. This flag remained in use until the republic's amalgamation into the USSR in 1940. The yellow band symbolises ripening wheat and consequently agricultural wealth and freedom from want. Green recalls the country's forests, and hope, while red represents love of the country, as well as referring to the colour of the old banners of the medieval kingdom of Lithuania. The tricolour began to reappear in public in early 1990, prior to the disintegration of the USSR.

# LUXEMBOURG

*Western Europe*

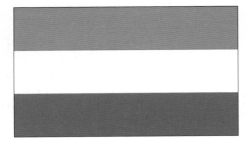

**Grand Duchy of Luxembourg**
**Flag ratio 3:5**

The colours of the grand duchy's flag derive directly
from its arms, which are centuries old: a shield which
forms the centrepiece of the arms has a blue-and-
white-striped background, with a red, crowned, two-
tailed lion rampant in the centre, and these colours
were adopted for the flag. Its design dates from the
mid-19th century and was probably influenced by
the French tricolour, but the flag itself was not officially
adopted until 1972. It is similar in appearance to the
flag of the Netherlands, but the Luxembourg blue
is of a paler shade and the flags' proportions are
slightly different.

*Eastern Europe*

# MACEDONIA

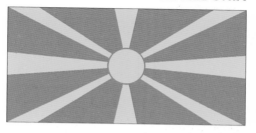

**Republic of Macedonia**
**Flag ratio 1:2**

The Yugoslavian province of Macedonia declared independence in 1992 but immediately found itself disagreeing with neighbouring Greece over its emblem, the Star of Vergina. It had become a popular emblem among Australian Macedonians, and was preferred for the new national flag over the traditional colours of black and red. It was said to derive from a decoration on the gold coffin of the Greek king Philip II of Macedon, father of Alexander the Great, and a version is also used as the emblem of the Greek province of Macedonia. The issue was resolved in 1995 after a treaty with Greece and the adoption of a modified sunburst motif for the flag to replace the star.

# MADAGASCAR

*Southern Africa (Indian Ocean)*

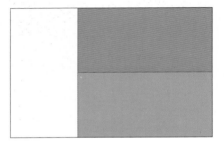

**Democratic Republic of Madagascar**
**Flag ratio 2:3**

Madagascar, a large island in the western Indian Ocean off the southeast coast of Africa, has been a traditional destination for immigrants from Southeast Asia, and this demographic trend is reflected in the colours of its flag. The red and white are said to represent the island's first inhabitants: the Hova people from Southeast Asia (red and white are the colours traditionally associated with the region; see, for example, the flag of Indonesia), as well as the Africans of the island. The green is said to represent the people of the coastal region; this colour was added when the flag was adopted in 1958, two years before full independence from France was gained.

*Southern Africa*

# MALAWI

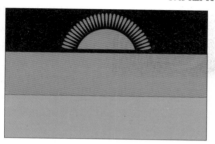

**Republic of Malawi**

**Flag ratio 2:3**

The ruling Malawi Congress Party used its flag, a horizontal tricolour of black, red and green, as the basis for the design of the new national flag when the country became independent in 1964. Its colours are symbolic: black, to represent the African people; red, for the blood of the freedom fighters; and green, to symbolise the land and its fertility. The rising sun was added to the black band in 1964 to symbolise a new dawn for Malawi and for Africa, and is based on the sun which appears, also against a black background, on the Malawi coat of arms.

# MALAYSIA

*Eastern Asia*

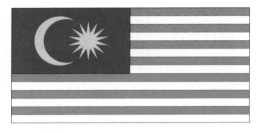

**Federation of Malaysia**

**Flag ratio 1:2**

At first sight, the Malaysian national flag is reminiscent of the Stars and Stripes, and this was the likely design inspiration, although the use of colours is probably coincidental. Red and white are traditionally used in Southeast Asia, while the blue stands for the unity of the Malaysian people. Yellow is the royal colour of the rulers of Malaysia, while the symbols represent the dominant religion, Islam. The Malaysian Federation's original 14 member states are represented in the 14 stripes and in the 14 points of the star. Singapore left the federation in 1965, two years after its founding, but the flag stayed the same, with the extra stripe and point now representing the federal government.

*Western Asia (Indian Ocean)* **MALDIVES**

**Republic of Maldives**
**Flag ratio 2:3**
The Maldives are a coral atoll in the Indian Ocean comprising over 1,000 islands; the local name for the group is The Thousand Islands. As with the flags of other states in the region, the colour red features prominently; in fact, the original flag of the islands had only a plain red field. The islands, which had been a British protectorate since 1887, became independent in 1965, and the present design was adopted in the same year. The colours represent the sacrifice of the heroes of the independence struggle (red), and progress and prosperity (green). The central panel contains a white crescent, recognised as a symbol of the Islamic religion.

# MALI

*West Africa*

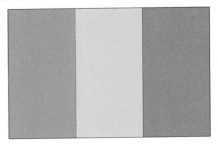

**Republic of Mali**
**Flag ratio 2:3**
Mali was a French colony from the late 19th century.
Before independence it formed the Mali Federation
with Senegal. Before independence it formed the Mali Federation
with Senegal. At independence in 1960, Senegal left
the federation. The flag is based on the French
tricolour in style and the green-yellow-red Pan-
African colours. These were used by many former
African colonies and express the wish for African
unity. The same basic flag has been used since 1959,
but at first it had a black human figure, the *kanaga*,
in the centre. This was removed from the flag in 1961.

*Western Europe (Mediterranean)*    **MALTA**

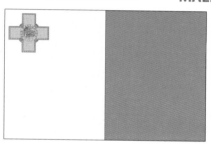

**Republic of Malta**
**Flag ratio 2:3**

Tradition states the national colours of white and red,
deriving from part of the pennant of the Hautevilles,
were given to the Maltese in 1090 by Count Roger
the Norman in thanks for the hospitality shown him
when he came to expel the Arabs. The red-fimbriated
George Cross in the canton was added in 1943 after
the medal's award to the islanders for heroism in
withstanding the Axis powers' three-year siege.
A blue canton set behind the cross was dropped
in 1964 when Malta became independent after
150 years of British rule. The traditional four-armed,
eight-pointed Maltese Cross appears in white on a
red field to form the civil ensign.

# MARSHALL ISLANDS

*Pacific Ocean*

**Republic of the Marshall Islands**
**Flag ratio 1:2**
Formerly a part of the United States Trust Territory
of the Pacific Islands, the Marshall Islands split from
Micronesia to become independent and in 1979
came both a new government and new flag. As with
other Pacific island states' flags, blue and white are
the main colours and a star motif features. The star
represents the islands themselves, and its 24 points
the islands' districts. The four elongated compass
points of the star express the islanders' Christian
faith, while the star's position, in a field of blue and
above the two bands, suggest their location, in the
Pacific Ocean slightly north of the equator. The white
and orange stripes represent hope and wealth.

*North Africa* **MAURITANIA**

**Islamic Republic of Mauritania**

**Flag ratio 2:3**

As with the other former French colonies of North Africa, Mauritania chose not to use the tricolour as the basis of its flag and instead elected to depict the predominance of the Muslim religion in the country. The crescent and five-pointed star are traditional Islamic motifs, as is the colour green which appears in the field. They also reflect the country's appellation of an Islamic republic. The flag was adopted in 1959, the year before Mauritania won its independence from France.

# MAURITIUS

*Indian Ocean*

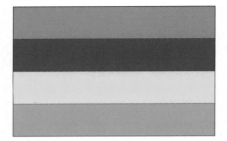

**Republic of Mauritius**

**Flag ratio 2:3**

The colours of the flag of Mauritius are those which appear on its coat of arms, which dates from 1906. The flag was adopted in 1968 on independence from Britain, which had ruled the island since 1815. The colours are said to have a particular significance: red represents the country's independence; blue is the colour of the Indian Ocean; yellow is for the country's bright future; and green stands for its lush vegetation. Although red, yellow and green are also the colours of the Pan-African movement, the adoption of those colours for use in national flags has largely been a Central and Western African practice, so it is unlikely that they carry the same significance here.

*Central America*

# MEXICO

**United Mexican States**

**Flag ratio 4:7**

The flag of Mexico was based on the French tricolour, a ubiquitous symbol of liberty. The colours were those of the movement for independence from Spain, and are also said to represent the three guarantees given by the freedom fighters: freedom of religious worship; independence from Spain; and the unity of the states of Mexico. The tricolour became the national flag on independence in 1821. The central emblem is the national arms, added in their present form in 1968. They depict an eagle on a cactus holding a snake in its beak, and reflect an Aztec legend of the founding of Mexico City, in which the place to be built upon would be signified by an eagle perching on a cactus.

# MICRONESIA

*Pacific Ocean*

**Federated States of Micronesia**

**Flag ratio 10:19**

When the Marshall Islands and Palau broke away from the original United States Trust Territory of Micronesia in 1979, the country was renamed the Federated States of Micronesia and a new flag was adopted. The old one had been based on the field of blue of the United Nations flag, as the islands had been entrusted to the United States of America by the UN; six stars represented the original six areas of the islands. The four stars of the current flag represent the members left in the federation: Kosrae, Pohnpei, Truk and Yap. Each of the separate states also has its own flag.

*Eastern Europe*                          # MOLDOVA

**Republic of Moldova**

**Flag ratio 1:2**

The flag of the new Republic of Moldova was adopted in late 1990, shortly before the official break-up of the old USSR. It bears a resemblance to the flag of Romania, and the central arms, featuring a spread eagle, are not unlike those previously used by the Romanians. Here, the bull's head symbolises Moldova, while the colours represent the past, present and future of the country as well as its democratic principles and historical traditions, and the equality of all its citizens.

# MONACO

*Western Europe*

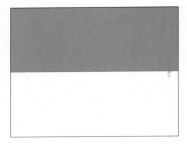

**Principality of Monaco**

**Flag ratio 4:5**

The Grimaldi family became rulers of Monaco in the 13th century and are still in power today. The state's relations with France and Italy have always been close but Monaco has retained its independence, and a constitution was established in 1911. The colours of the flag are taken from the ruling family's coat of arms, which are of medieval origin: the central shield of the arms is covered by red and white lozenges, or diamonds. The flag was adopted in 1881 and is distinguished from the similar red-over-white bicolour of Indonesia by its squarer proportions.

*Eastern Asia*  **MONGOLIA**

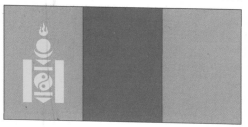

Mongolia
**Flag ratio 1:2**
Nationalism and Buddhism are represented in the
Mongolian flag. The red bands originally represented
Communism. Now they symbolise prosperity and
progress. The central blue band is a traditional colour
of the Mongol peoples, and represents patriotism.
The gold *Soyonbo* at the hoist is a Buddhist symbol,
in which the shapes represent aspects of the
Buddhist faith, eternal life (the sun and moon), and
the balance of life (the yin-yang symbol). It also stands
for the independence, spirit and sovereignty of
Mongolia. The flag was adopted in 1940. On the fall
of Communism the *Soyonbo* was changed to remove
the Communist star, which had appeared above it.

# MONTSERRAT

*Caribbean*

**Colony of Montserrat**
**Flag ratio 1:2**
Although Montserrat, one of the Leeward Islands, was first discovered by Christopher Columbus in 1493, its main European settlers were not Iberian, but Irish. Irish settlers began arriving in the 1630s but the island ultimately fell to Britain and remains a British colony (see corner flag). Both its British and Irish connections are reflected in its flag. The Blue Ensign bears, in its fly, the island arms: a shield depicting a woman in green holding a gold harp. The figure represents Ireland, and the cross she embraces, the people's love of Christ and Catholicism. The arms date from 1909.

*North Africa*

# MOROCCO

**Kingdom of Morocco**
**Flag ratio 2:3**
Red has been the traditional colour of the flag of Morocco since the 16th century, and is said to represent the blood ties between the royal family and the prophet Mohammed. The green pentacle, depicting the Seal of Solomon, was added to the centre in 1915, and the flag has remained in its present form since then. Like other French-occupied areas and colonies in northern Africa, but unlike those to the south, Morocco has not taken any adaptation of the tricolour to use as its flag. Even during French occupation, the only evidence was a tricolour in the canton of the civil ensign.

# MOZAMBIQUE

*Southern Africa*

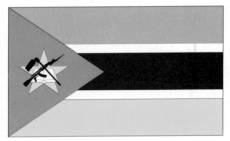

**Republic of Mozambique**

**Flag ratio 5:8**

Mozambique's flag is based on that of its main political party, FRELIMO, who led the country to freedom from Portugal in 1975. The colours are symbolic: green for the land and its riches, black for the African continent, and gold for mineral wealth. The red triangle at the hoist stands for the fight for freedom, and the two white fimbriations are for peace. The emblem of an open book under a crossed rifle and hoe stands for teachers and education, the army and the fight for freedom, and the economic importance of agricultural work. They are backed by the five-pointed gold star of Communism and internationalism. This modified version of the original flag was adopted in 1983.

*Eastern Asia*

# MYANMAR

**Union of Myanmar**

**Flag ratio 5:9**

The flag of Myanmar (formerly Burma) is based on a World War II resistance flag, which had a red field and a white star in the canton. A blue canton and five small stars around the large one, showing ethnic diversity and national unity, were added at independence in 1948. The flag changed in 1974 under Communist rule. The five stars were increased to 14, for the 14 states of the country, forming a circle around a cogwheel and two ears of paddy, for industry and agriculture. The modern meaning of the colours is red for courage, blue for peace and integrity, and white for purity and virtue. The country's name was changed in 1989 from Burma to Myanmar, although many people in the country and abroad still refer to it as Burma.

# NAMIBIA

*Southern Africa*

**Republic of Namibia**
**Flag ratio 2:3**
Formerly the trust territory of South West Africa, Namibia was occupied by South Africa until 1990. The national flag adopted on independence was based on the winner of a competition and uses the colours found in the flags of certain Namibian political parties. Blue symbolises the sky, the Atlantic Ocean and the importance of water and rain; red represents the Namibian people and their aspiration of a fair and equitable society; and green stands for vegetation and agricultural resources. The white fimbriations symbolise peace and unity, while the sun depicts life and energy, and its gold colour the sun's warmth, the golden plains and colour of the desert.

*Pacific Ocean*

# NAURU

**Republic of Nauru**
**Flag ratio 1:2**
In common with the flags of some other Pacific
island nations, the flag of Nauru depicts the nation's
geographical location. Represented by the star, Nauru
appears set in the Pacific Ocean just to the south
of the equator. The 12 points of the star are said to
represent the 12 indigenous tribes of the island.
The flag was adopted on independence from the
joint administration of Australia, New Zealand and
Britain in 1968, and was the winning entry in a
competition.

# NEPAL

*Southern Asia*

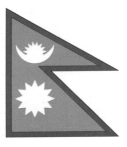

**Kingdom of Nepal**

**Flag ratio 4:3 along straight edges**

The flag of Nepal is the only national flag which is not rectangular, being based upon two separate pennants, flown one above the other, which belonged to rival branches of the Rana dynasty, the former rulers of Nepal. The two pennants were first joined in the last century, but the flag was not adopted officially until 1962, after the establishment of a constitutional form of government. The white sun and horizontal crescent moon are now said to express the hope that Nepal itself will last as long as the sun and moon. These motifs appear in white against a red background (crimson being the national colour), and a blue border edges the whole flag.

*Western Europe*

# NETHERLANDS

**Kingdom of the Netherlands**

**Flag ratio 2:3**

Possibly the first revolutionary tricolour, the Dutch
flag of red, white and blue may have been used as
a model for the French tricolour, itself a seminal
influence on flags throughout the world. The flag was
first used in the late 16th century in the struggle for
independence from the ruling Spanish Hapsburg
Empire. The colours were originally orange, white
and blue but changed to red, white and blue in the
mid-17th century and probably came from the livery
and arms of William of Orange, main leader of the
independence movement: a blue hunting horn with
silver mountings, hanging on a red cord.

# NETHERLANDS ANTILLES  *Caribbean*

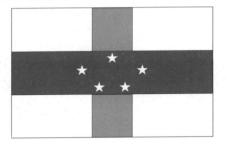

**Netherlands Antilles**
**Flag ratio 2:3**

A self-governing territory of the Netherlands (see corner flag), the Antilles are two island groups in the Caribbean which became part of the Dutch Empire in the 17th century. They became autonomous in 1954, and the flag was adopted originally in 1959. The red and blue bands of the Netherlands have been used, in a cross pattern on a white field, while the five stars represent the islands themselves: Bonaire, Curaçao, Saba, St Eustatius and St Maarten. There were formerly six stars, the sixth representing Aruba, but that island became self-governing in 1986. The other islands, except St Eustatius, now have their own flags.

*Australasia*

# NEW ZEALAND

**New Zealand**

**Flag ratio 1:2**

New Zealand's recent history as a colony of Britain is reflected in the appearance of its flag, which is based on the British Blue Ensign, with the country's distinguishing badge set in the fly: a group of four white-fimbriated, red five-pointed stars, a stylised representation of the Southern Cross constellation and a design feature commonly found on the flags of many countries in the southern hemisphere. This flag had originally been designed in 1869 for use at sea, and was officially adopted as the national flag on land in 1902, around the time that Australia was adopting a similar flag.

# NICARAGUA

*Central America*

**Republic of Nicaragua**
**Flag ratio 3:5**
Nicaragua was a member of the United Provinces
(1821–38). The flags of all five states are based on the
federation tribar and the modern Salvadorean and
Nicaraguan flags differ only in shades of colour and
central detail. Blue above and below white show the
Caribbean Sea and the Pacific Ocean to the north
and south of Central America. The arms on the state
flag are derived from the United Provinces arms.
They are a triangle for justice and equality, containing
an isthmus with five peaks (for the five provinces)
between two seas. The cap of liberty is for freedom
and the rainbow for hope. Around are the name of
the country and 'America Central'.

*West Africa*

# NIGER

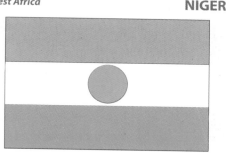

**Republic of Niger**
**Flag ratio 2:3**

Niger, like other former French colonies, used the
tricolour as a design model for its own flag on
independence. It was part of French West Africa from
the beginning of this century until 1960, and the
present flag was adopted in 1959 in anticipation of
independence the following year. The colours symbolise
the country's physical features: orange represents the
Sahara Desert which occupies much of the north
of the country, green the grasslands of the south,
and white the River Niger flowing between the two.
The orange disc in the centre symbolises the sun.
Côte d'Ivoire, also once a part of French West Africa,
is the only other African country using these colours.

# NIGERIA

*West Africa*

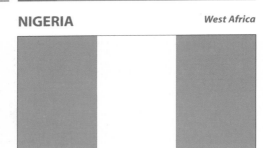

**Federal Republic of Nigeria**

**Flag ratio 1:2**

Nigeria was a British colony from the 19th century until 1960, when the flag of the new nation was adopted. The present flag was the winning entry in a competition held in 1959. The green–white–green vertical tribar depicts the country. The River Niger, shown by the white band, runs through forests on either side represented by the green. In addition, green represents agriculture, Nigeria's main source of wealth, and the white symbolises unity and peace.

*Pacific Ocean*

# NIUE

**Niue**

**Flag ratio 1:2**

The flag of Niue is based on that of New Zealand, of whom the island has been an autonomous dependency (see corner flag) since 1974. The flag itself was adopted in 1975. The yellow field represents the warmth of mutual friendship between Niue and New Zealand. The four five-pointed stars of the Southern Cross constellation, on the fly of the New Zealand flag, appear in yellow on the arms of the Cross of St George in the Union Jack in the canton, and the central yellow star, set within a blue disc, represents Niue itself. Many Pacific Ocean nations choose to represent themselves in their flags by the use of stars.

# NORTH KOREA

*Eastern Asia*

**Democratic People's Republic of North Korea**
**Flag ratio 1:2**
Korea was a united kingdom for over 500 years until the Japanese annexation in 1910. Liberation in 1945 meant more occupation, this time by Soviet and US forces north and south of the 38th parallel. The Soviets withdrew in 1948 but North Korea's government remained Communist, a fact shown in its flag. The flag was also adopted in 1948 and uses the blue, red and white of the traditional Korean standard, set in a new pattern. Three blue, red and blue bands are separated by two narrower white ones. In the red band, towards the hoist and in a white roundel, is the red, five-pointed Communist star. There have been moves recently to reunify the two parts of Korea.

*Pacific Ocean*  # NORTHERN MARIANAS

**Northern Marianas**
**Flag ratio 10:19**

The field of blue and prominent white star mark out this as the flag of a Pacific state, as the flags of several countries in the region share these characteristics. The blue is derived from the UN flag, as Northern Marianas was formerly a trust territory of the UN, administered by the US after years of Japanese occupation. Northern Marianas broke away from the sprawling US Pacific Trust Territory in 1976, and its flag was adopted that year. The white star, representing the islands, appears in front of a chalice-shaped stone icon, a Polynesian *taga*, a symbol of authority. It represents the ancient culture and traditions of the people and is surrounded by a flower garland.

# NORWAY

*Scandinavia*

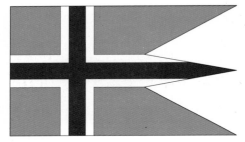

**Kingdom of Norway**
**Flag ratio 8:11**

The off-centre cross shows Norway's links with the Norse countries. Norway was ruled by Denmark from 1397 until 1814, then by Sweden. Despite an active 19th-century nationalist movement, the union with Sweden was not dissolved until 1905. General use of the flag was not allowed by the Swedes until the late 19th century. The addition of the blue cross over the white Danish one was a reference to the red, white and blue of the US and the UK, as countries which were not ruled by an absolute monarch. They also referred to the colours of France, by then recognised as revolutionary colours. As in Finland and Sweden, the modern naval ensign is swallowtailed with a tongue.

**Middle East**

# OMAN

**Sultanate of Oman**

**Flag ratio 1:2**

The accession of Sultan Quabus bin Sa'id in 1970 saw the adoption of a new Omani flag. Until then, the country (called Muscat and Oman) had used the centuries-old red banner of the indigenous peoples, the Kharijite Muslims. Red has been retained in the new flag, now with the addition of white and green panels in the upper and lower parts of the fly. In the canton appear the state arms in red and white: two crossed sabres feature behind a *gambia*, a traditional local dagger, and an elaborate horse bit appears in the foreground over all.

# PAKISTAN

*Southern Asia*

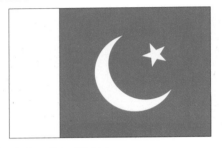

**Islamic Republic of Pakistan**
**Flag ratio 2:3**
The flag of Pakistan, officially adopted in 1947, is based on the flag of the All-India Muslim League, a body which spearheaded the struggle of South Asia Muslims for a separate Muslim state. Pakistan gained independence in 1947 when India was partitioned into two separate dominions on British withdrawal, and it became an Islamic Republic in 1956. The national flag is green with a white vertical bar at the hoist, a white central crescent and a five-pointed white star. The white and green together stand for peace and prosperity, the crescent progress, and the five-rayed star light and knowledge. The green, the star and the crescent are also traditional Islamic motifs.

*Pacific Ocean*

# PALAU

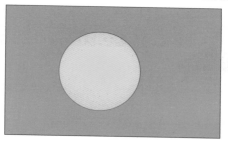

**Republic of Palau**
**Flag ratio 13:15**
Originally part of the United States Trust Territory of the Pacific Islands, Palau broke away to become a self-governing republic in 1981. The flag dates from the same period. The blue field is common to the flags of many nations in this area of the world, and represents their location in the Pacific. The yellow disc, set slightly towards the hoist, represents the full moon and is a symbol of productiveness. It is also a reference to the ancient culture of the islanders and their belief that the time of the full moon is the most productive for creative tasks like planting, harvesting and fishing.

# PALESTINE

*Middle East*

**Palestine National Authority**

**Flag ratio 1:2**

The flag of Palestine is in the traditional Pan-Arab colours, and is very close in design to the flag of the early 20th-century Arab Revolt, from which the colours originate. The four dynasties of the Arabian caliphs are represented in the flag: black stands for both the dark past of the Palestinian people and the Abbasid dynasty; white represents the purity of the Muslim faith and the Umayyad dynasty; green is the traditional colour representing Islam, and also here the Fatimid dynasty; and red is for courage and the Hashemite dynasty. At present the flag is not recognised internationally, as there is not a fully independent Palestinian state.

*Central America*

# PANAMA

**Republic of Panama**

**Flag ratio 2:3**

In 1903 Panama was a province of Colombia. Colombia and the US were engaged in talks over the building of a canal to link the Pacific and the Caribbean. Colombia refused the US permission to do so. As a result, Panama seceded and allowed the US to build the canal. The flag was designed by the first president, made overnight by his wife, and hoisted when the country declared independence. Blue was for the Conservative Party and red for the Liberal Party, while white was for peace and cooperation between them. The blue star is for public honesty and loyalty, and the red star for the supremacy of the law.

# PAPUA NEW GUINEA

*Australasia*

**Papua New Guinea**
**Flag ratio 3:4**
Papua New Guinea unites the once-German territory
of New Guinea with Australian-administered Papua.
The country gained independence in 1975. The
distinctive national flag has triangles of red over black.
The 'kumul bird' of paradise, unique to the country
and first used as an emblem in the 19th century, flies
across the red half, showing PNG's emergence into
nationhood. The stars of the Southern Cross on the
black reflect ties with Australia and other South Pacific
nations. Black, red and yellow are traditional colours
among the people of the country. The flag was
designed by a 15-year-old schoolgirl, and was
adopted in 1971.

**South America**

# PARAGUAY

**Republic of Paraguay**

**Flag ratio 1:2**

Paraguay's flag is unusual because it has different badges on its obverse (above) and reverse sides. The red, white and blue horizontal tricolour first appeared in 1811 on independence from Spain. It was probably influenced by the French tricolour. The present version, with new central emblems, has been used since 1842. The obverse emblem depicts the Star of May, used as a symbol of freedom and independence on South American flags, and here a symbol of Paraguayan freedom from Spain (achieved on 14 May 1811). On the reverse is the seal of the treasury, showing a lion guarding a staff on which is a cap of liberty, with the words *Paz y Justicia* ('Peace and Justice') above.

# PERU

*South America*

**Republic of Peru**
**Flag ratio 2:3**

The traditional explanation of this tribar as the Peruvian national flag is whimsical: in 1821, General José de San Martín, fighting to free the country from Spanish rule, saw a flock of flamingoes, with white breasts and red wings, fly over his troops. He took it for a good omen, and declared red and white to be the colours of liberty. The story's accuracy is not known, but red and white were also associated with the local Inca peoples. The flag was officially adopted in 1825 after the defeat of Spain. The addition of the national arms to the centre forms the state flag. These comprise a shield with three motifs of local flora, fauna and natural resources, surrounded by a wreath.

*Eastern Asia*

# PHILIPPINES

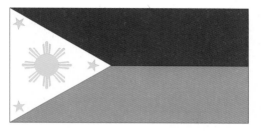

**Republic of the Philippines**
**Flag ratio 1:2**

The Philippine flag had its origins in the liberation movement against Spain in the 1890s. It may have been inspired by the American flag, and was used in 1898 when the islands fell to America after the Spanish-American War. The white triangle in the hoist represents the liberation movement, while the blue and red bands represent magnanimity and courage respectively. The colours are reversed in time of war. The large, eight-pointed yellow star in the triangle's centre commemorates the eight provinces who rose in revolt against Spain, while the yellow stars at the triangle's points stand for the three main island groups: Luzon, Mindanao and the Visayan archipelago.

# PITCAIRN ISLANDS     *Pacific Ocean*

**Colony of the Pitcairn Islands**
**Flag ratio 1:2**

Pitcairn Island was the place chosen by several of the mutineers from HMS *Bounty* as their home in 1790, and this is one of the elements represented in the island's flag. The blue field represents the Pacific Ocean, the green triangle Pitcairn itself and the gold edging around the island's beaches. Set within the triangle are a Bible, representing the importance of Christianity, and the anchor of the *Bounty*. The crest is a wheelbarrow and a food plant to show the traditional importance of agriculture. The arms themselves date from 1969 but the flag was adopted more recently, in 1983. The Islands are a British Colony (see corner flag).

*Eastern Europe*

# POLAND

**Republic of Poland**
**Flag ratio 5:8**

The colours of white and red which form this flag
are derived from the national arms, in use since the
13th century. These depict a white eagle on a red
field, and while the national flag is plain, other official
flags bear the national arms. The national rising of
1830–31 against the Russians (Poland being part of
the Russian Empire at this time) saw the adoption of
red and white cockades by the insurgents, although
the colours were proscribed after the rising was put
down. The red and white flag was officially adopted
in 1919, when Poland was reformed in the Versailles
settlement, having been partitioned by the major
powers in the previous two centuries.

# PORTUGAL

*Western Europe*

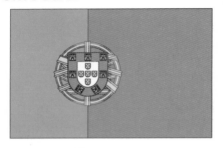

**Portuguese Republic**
**Flag ratio 2:3**

Portugal's flag dates from 1910. Red and green were
the colours for the new republic, while the central
emblem was the traditional Portuguese arms. The
white shield with five small blue shields represents
the victory of King Afonso Henriques over five
Moorish princes in 1139. The five white dots on each
shield recall the five wounds of Christ. The seven gold
castles in the red orle (border to the shield) refer to
the marriage of King Afonso III to a Spanish princess
in 1252. The armillary sphere recalls the Portuguese
role in exploring the globe. Used in slightly different
forms under the kingdom, the present form was
adopted for the new flag in 1910.

*Caribbean*

# PUERTO RICO

**Commonwealth of Puerto Rico**
**Flag ratio 2:3**

At first glance the Puerto Rican flag looks identical to Cuba's, with just the red and blue transposed. Both flags express a common aspiration of the islands in the 19th century – freedom from Spanish rule with the help of the US. The flag of Puerto Rico came later than Cuba's, and was based intentionally on it, being used by the revolutionaries during their attempts to win independence from 1895 onwards. The island fell to the US after the Spanish-American War of 1898, and although it became self-governing in 1952 – when the flag was adopted officially – it remains a dependent territory (see corner flag) and so flies its flag only alongside the Stars and Stripes.

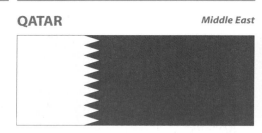

# QATAR

*Middle East*

**State of Qatar**
**Flag ratio 11:28**
The flag of Qatar is similar to that of Bahrain, with which the country was once linked. The peoples of both countries are Kharijite Muslims, whose traditional banner was red. It is believed that the present maroon colour came about from the action of the elements, especially the sun, on the natural red dyes once used for the flag. Like Bahrain, Qatar has a zigzag white interlock at the hoist, deriving from a British request in 1820 that all friendly states around the Arabian Gulf add a white band to their flags. The flag assumed its present form around the mid-19th century, and was officially adopted when Qatar became independent in 1971.

*Eastern Europe*                    **ROMANIA**

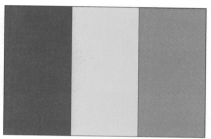

Romania

**Flag ratio 2:3**

The Romanian tricolour emerged in 1848, a year of
revolutions in Europe, to express the desire for freedom
from the Ottoman Empire. Its original design,
a horizontal tricolour, was probably, based on the
principles of liberty symbolised by the French tricolour.
The bands became vertical in 1867. The colours are
those of the provinces: blue and red for Moldavia, and
blue and yellow for Wallachia. From 1867 until 1990,
emblems appeared in the centre – first royalist, then
Communist – but since the over-throw of Communism
the flag has been plain, making it identical to Chad's.
In 2003 the addition of the current arms to the flag
was approved but no date has been set for this.

# RUSSIA

*Eastern Europe*

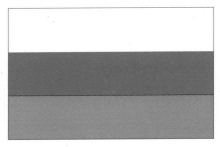

**Russian Federation**
**Flag ratio 2:3**
The tricolour of Russia dates from the time of reforming Tsar Peter the Great (1672–1725) who travelled in Europe towards the end of the 17th century, and spent some time in Amsterdam and Leiden. The colours and design of the Dutch flag were adopted and rearranged to form a white, blue and red pattern. The tricolour was not adopted officially until 1799 and fell into disuse after the Bolshevik revolution of 1917, being revived as the Russian flag in 1990 as the USSR disintegrated. The colours and design of the flag had a great influence on the Pan-Slav movement in Eastern Europe in the 19th century, with many small nations adopting them as their own.

*Central Africa*

# RWANDA

**Republic of Rwanda**

**Flag ratio 2:3**

When Rwanda gained independence from Belgium in 1962, it adopted a vertical tricolour of red, yellow and green. To distinguish it from the flag of Guinea, a black letter 'R' was added in the centre. The country fell into serious civil war in 1997, in which many people were killed. On 31 December 2001, Rwanda adopted a new flag. The upper half is light blue and the lower divided equally yellow over green. Blue is for peace and tranquillity after the violence of recent years. Yellow is for wealth and for economic growth. Green is for prosperity, work and productivity. At the outer end of the blue panel is a 24-rayed yellow sun for new hope and light.

## ST HELENA

*S Atlantic Ocean*

**Colony of St Helena and Dependencies**
**Flag ratio 1:2**
The island of St Helena lies in the Atlantic Ocean,
west of Africa. It was taken over by the English East
India Company in 1659, but became a British Crown
Colony in 1834 (see corner flag). Its dependencies
are the islands of Ascension and Tristan da Cunha.
St Helena was the island to which Napoleon was
exiled after the Battle of Waterloo in 1815, and
where he died in 1821. The flag is the usual British
Blue Ensign with the colonial badge. The badge
shows a ship of the East India Company approaching
the rocky shores of the island. In the yellow chief
above the ship is a wirebird, found only on the island.

*Caribbean*

# ST KITTS AND NEVIS

**Federation of St Kitts and Nevis**
**Flag ratio 2:3**

St Kitts and Nevis, former British colonies, gained independence in 1983, and this flag was adopted that year. It was the winning entry in a local competition and uses colours found in other West Indian flags. Green, yellow and red are also the colours of the Pan-African movement, although in this context the colours officially have a different significance: green represents the islands' fertility; red stands for the struggles of the people from slavery through colonialism to independence; and yellow is for the sunshine. The peoples' African heritage is acknowledged by the black, while the two white stars symbolise hope and liberty.

# ST LUCIA

*Caribbean*

**State of St Lucia**
**Flag ratio 1:2**
The flag design which St Lucia used while an associated state was retained after the island's independence from Britain in 1979. The flag is a stylised depiction of St Lucia itself: a volcanic island amid a blue sea, with three central mountains, the Pitons, in the centre. The colours are symbolic in themselves: blue stands for fidelity, as well as for the Caribbean and the Atlantic surrounding the shores; gold stands for prosperity and sunshine; and black and white represent dual racial culture and harmony. The design was the winning entry in a locally held competition.

*Caribbean*

# ST VINCENT AND THE GRENADINES

**St Vincent and the Grenadines**
**Flag ratio 2:3**
In common with the flags of other West Indian states, that of St Vincent emerged as the winner in a local competition. The flag in use at present is a modified version of the original. The bands of colour are symbolic: blue for the sky, yellow for the sunshine, and green for the islands' lush vegetation. The 'V' of diamonds in the centre stands for 'Vincent'; this was introduced in 1985 to replace the previous central motif of a breadfruit leaf behind the islands' arms. The original version had been adopted in 1979 when the islands became independent from Britain.

# SAMOA

*Pacific Ocean*

**Independent State of Samoa**
**Flag ratio 1:2**
Samoa passed from German control after World War I
to be administered by New Zealand as a trust territory.
In the islands' first flag, adopted in 1948, the cross in
the canton had four stars, like the New Zealand flag,
but this became five in 1949, and this design was
kept when the islands became independent in 1962.
Red and white were traditionally used in Samoan
flags, but now red is said to stand for the blood shed
in the independence struggle and blue for national
unity. Like other southern hemisphere countries,
Samoa's flag bears the distinctive Southern Cross
constellation and here it indicates the islands'
location in the Pacific.

*Western Europe*

# SAN MARINO

**Republic of San Marino**
**Flag ratio 3:4**

Reputedly founded in the 4th century AD, San Marino
is the world's smallest republic. The colours of its flag
are said to represent the snowy peaked mountains
and sky, and they also feature in the national arms
which appear in the centre of the official state flag.
A heart-shaped shield, topped by a crown (a symbol
of authority), contains three towers with ostrich
plumes above. These depict the three towers built
on Mount Titano, the main mountain in San Marino,
and symbolise the republic's ability to defend itself.
A laurel and oak wreath surround these, with the
motto, *Libertas*, below, another reminder of the state's
independence.

# SÃO TOMÉ AND PRINCIPE *West Africa*

**Democratic Republic of São Tomé and Principe**
**Flag ratio 1:2**
The flag of the main liberation movement, the
Movimento de Liberación de São Tomé e Principe
(MLSP), was adopted in 1975 as the national flag of
this former Portuguese colony, with a modification
to the proportions of the bands. Red, green and
yellow are the colours of the Pan-African movement,
symbolising African solidarity and nationalism. They
were adopted by many former colonies, particularly
in West Africa, on their liberation. The two black stars
represent the islands themselves and their African
peoples.

*Middle East*

# SAUDI ARABIA

**Kingdom of Saudi Arabia**

**Flag ratio 2:3**

The Saudi Arabian flag is distinctive in both simplicity of design and in featuring an inscription as the central motif. The inscription reads, 'There is no god but Allah, and Mohammed is the Prophet of Allah'. This is the *shahada*, or Muslim creed. Two copies of the flag are sewn back-to-back so that the inscription may be read correctly on both sides. The hilt of the sword is in both cases to the fly. The sword commemorates the victories of Ibn Saud which unified the kingdom with its present boundaries in the early 20th century. Green represents both Islam and the Wahhabi sect, the predominant branch of Islam in Saudi Arabia.

# SCOTLAND

*Western Europe*

**Scotland**

**Flag ratio 3:5**

The now official national flag of Scotland is the 'Cross of St Andrew' or Saltire. Traditionally, St Andrew was martyred on an X-shaped cross, as he said he was not worthy to die as Christ had done. He later became the patron saint of Scotland, and the diagonal cross represents him. The colours are from a legend which states that the Scots won a battle after a white diagonal cross appeared in the sky, probably a cloud formation. This has been the Scottish emblem since the 14th century. When the Union Flag was designed in 1606, this was the basis, as King James was King of Scotland before he was also King of England. The Saltire was adopted officially as the flag of Scotland by the Scottish Parliament at its first meeting.

*West Africa*

# SENEGAL

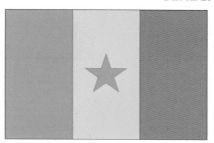

**Republic of Senegal**
**Flag ratio 2:3**
Senegal, in federation with neighbouring Mali, became independent of France in 1960, then left the federation. Senegal retained the basic flag of the federation, a tricolour based on that of France, but in the Pan-African colours of green, yellow and red. These show solidarity with other African states. The black *kanaga* figure which appeared in the Mali flag was removed from the centre and replaced with a green star, to represent the opening of Senegal to the five continents. The flag was officially adopted in 1960 and has remained unchanged.

# SERBIA AND MONTENEGRO

*Eastern Europe*

**Serbia and Montenegro**

**Flag ratio 1:2**

Serbia and Montenegro were the first southern Slav states to gain independence. Serbia and Montenegro, part of the Pan-Slav movement, chose the Russian colours. They inverted the Russian flag into red–blue–white. To distinguish them, Montenegro added the initials of its king. After World War I, Serbia, Montenegro, Bosnia-Herzegovina, Macedonia, Croatia and Slovenia united to form Yugoslavia. A flag of blue, white and red was chosen because this combination was not used by any of the states. Under the post-World War II Communist regime, a red star edged gold was added. This was removed in 1992, when Yugoslavia disintegrated, leaving only Serbia and Montenegro to carry on the name 'Yugoslavia' until it was dropped in 2003.

*Indian Ocean*

# SEYCHELLES

**Republic of Seychelles**

**Flag ratio 1:2**

The Seychelles has had three flags in its short period of independence. The first lasted just a year, from 1976, before a coup. The new government, the People's United Party (later People's Progressive Front, or PPF), used their flag as the national one. But in 1996 one-party rule was abolished and a new flag adopted which was not just based on the PPF colours. Now the red band represents revolution and progress to a fair and equitable society; green is for agriculture, the islands' main source of wealth; blue and white depict the Indian Ocean around the archipelago; and yellow the natural and mineral resources in it. Together, the colours symbolise the islanders' unity and aspirations.

# SIERRA LEONE

*West Africa*

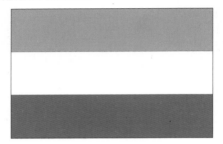

**Republic of Sierra Leone**
**Flag ratio 2:3**
Sierra Leone was the first African nation set up as a
haven for freed slaves, in 1787, although subsequently
it became a British colony. The national flag, a horizontal
tricolour of green, white and blue, symbolises various
aspects and attributes of the country. The green
band represents the country's agriculture, and the
characteristic vegetation of its wooded slopes;
the white stands for peace and justice; and the blue
symbolises the waters of the Atlantic. The flag was
adopted in 1961 when Sierra Leone became
independent of Britain.

*Eastern Asia*

# SINGAPORE

**Republic of Singapore**
**Flag ratio 2:3**
The red and white used in the Singapore flag are
colours which appear often in the flags of Southeast
Asia. In this instance, the red stands for universal
brotherhood and equality of man, and the white for
everlasting purity and virtue. The crescent represents
the young nation's ascent, guided by the five stars
of democracy, peace, progress, justice and equality.
It was adopted in 1959 when Singapore was still
a British colony and was retained when it became
independent in 1965, having joined and left the
Malaysian Federation in the intervening years.

# SLOVAKIA

*Eastern Europe*

**Republic of Slovakia**
**Flag ratio 2:3**
Slovakia's flag dates from 1848, a year of revolutions in Europe, and the time when Slav wishes for independence from the Austro-Hungarian Empire came to the fore. The flag is the Russian tricolour, with the addition of the national arms, set towards the hoist. A similar flag, although with the arms in the centre, was used from 1938, when Czechoslovakia was broken up, but it was abolished in 1945, when the country reunited. When Czechoslovakia finally split in 1993 the flag was restored, but with the arms again set towards the hoist. The arms, showing the Cross of Christianity on the Tatra Mountains, are the ancient emblem of the country.

*Eastern Europe*

# SLOVENIA

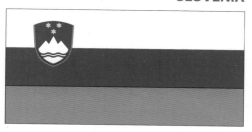

**Republic of Slovenia**

**Flag ratio 1:2**

The Slovenian flag's colours are the Pan-Slav white, blue and red. The flag, modelled on the Russian tricolour, originated in the 19th century as the Slav states were trying to win home rule from the Austro-Hungarian Empire. At the end of World War I in 1918 the southern Slav states were formed into the new state of Yugoslavia. But the decline of European Communism in the late 1980s removed the threads which had bound the disparate elements of the federation, and Slovenia and Croatia broke away from the Yugoslavian federation in 1991. Slovenia adopted the traditional tricolour, with the shield of arms in the canton, as its new national flag.

# SOLOMON ISLANDS   *Pacific Ocean*

**Solomon Islands**
**Flag ratio 1:2**
This flag was adopted in 1977 in anticipation of
independence the following year, after almost a
century of colonial rule, first by Germany and then
by Britain. Its colours are symbolic, representing the
sea (blue), the land (green) and sunshine (yellow).
The five stars represent the five districts into which
the islands were previously divided (there are now
eight districts, but this is not yet reflected in the flag).
The colours of the flag are also dominant in the
national arms which were adopted at the same time.

*East Africa*

# SOMALIA

**Somalia**

**Flag ratio 2:3**

Somalia was formed by a union in 1960 of British Somalia and Italian Somaliland, the latter a United Nations Trust Territory from 1950. The present flag was adopted by the Italian, southern part of the country in 1954 and is based on the colours of the UN flag. On the establishment of the unified state in 1960, it was adopted as the national flag. The star is a symbol of liberty, and its five points represent the five areas in which the Somali peoples live: the two former regions, now united; Djibouti; northern Kenya; and southern Ethiopia.

# SOUTH AFRICA

*Southern Africa*

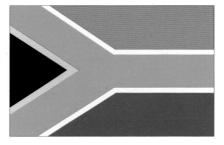

**Republic of South Africa**

**Flag ratio 2:3**

In 1994, when South Africa's non-racial constitution was inaugurated, its new flag was raised for the first time. This replaced the previous orange–white–blue horizontal tricolour in use since 1928. The present flag uses the colours of the country's main political and racial groupings. Black, yellow and green are the colours of the dominant African National Congress. Red, white, blue and green are from the former flags of the white Afrikaner republics. Black, green, yellow, red and white are from the Zulu Inkatha Freedom Party. Although this was intended as a temporary flag until a permanent constitution was accepted, there has been no change, and the flag seems destined to last.

*Eastern Asia* # SOUTH KOREA

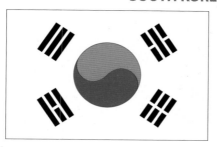

**Republic of South Korea**
**Flag ratio 2:3**
Based on a 19th-century flag of the united kingdom of Korea, this flag has been used in its present form since 1950, after the kingdom was partitioned. The white field represents the people's purity and desire for peace, while its central emblem is the red and blue yin-yang symbol, representing creation and development through duality and balance. Around this are four black trigrams, or *kwae* symbols, taken from the I Ching (the ancient Chinese book of divination and philosophy); they represent the four seasons, four compass points, four elements and the sun, moon, earth and heaven. They denote the process of yin and yang going through a spiral of change and growth.

# SPAIN

*Western Europe*

**Kingdom of Spain**

**Flag ratio 2:3**

The Spanish colours were adopted in 1785 by King
Charles III. The flag then included the arms of Castille
and León. In 1931 the Republic replaced this with a
red–yellow–purple horizontal tricolour. After the Civil
War, the Republic was abolished in 1939, and the red
and yellow were restored. The state flag (main image)
has the arms set towards the hoist. They show in a
shield the arms of five provinces, with the royal
Bourbon fleur-de-lys badge in the centre. Above is the
Spanish royal crown and on either side the Pillars of
Hercules, once believed to be the limits of the world.
The sea is at their base and the motto *Plus Ultra*
('More Beyond') recalls overseas exploration and
the former Spanish Empire in America.

*Southern Asia* # SRI LANKA

**Democratic Socialist Republic of Sri Lanka**
**Flag ratio 1:2**
This flag's design has evolved in an attempt to foster
national unity since the country, then called Ceylon,
gained independence from Britain in 1948. Originally
the central emblem was a gold lion and sword on
a red field, derived from the flag of the Sinhalese
kingdom of Kandy. It was consequently unpopular
with minority groups and in 1951 saw the additions
of green and orange bands, for the Muslim and Tamil
communities. Finally, when the country adopted the
local name of Sri Lanka in 1972, the flag was changed
again, with four leaves of the *pipul* tree, a Buddhist
symbol, added to the four corners of the dark red panel.
This version of the flag was in official use from 1978.

# SUDAN

*North Africa*

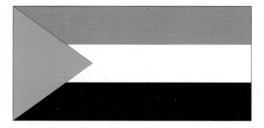

**Republic of Sudan**

**Flag ratio 1:2**

The Pan-Arab colours were adopted for the current flag of Sudan in 1970, after a revolution brought down the existing government and led to the abandoning of the national flag – a blue, yellow and green horizontal tricolour – used since independence from Anglo-Egyptian control in 1956. The new colours were expressive of Arab nationalism and were the colours of the new ruling party, but they were also intended to be of significance in their own right: red for the independence struggle; white for peace; black for the nation; and green for prosperity and the Islamic religion.

*South America*

# SURINAME

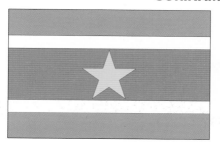

**Republic of Suriname**

**Flag ratio 2:3**

Suriname, formerly Dutch Guiana, gained independence in 1975 and its flag dates from then. It superseded an older flag, from 1959, of a white field with five stars in white, black, brown, yellow and red, representing the country's racial diversity. The colours of the three main political parties at the time of independence were used in the new flag, with the green, white and red now representing fertility, justice and freedom, and renewal respectively. The central feature, a gold star, symbolises national sacrifice, unity and hope for the nation's golden future. It echoes a yellow star in the centre of the national arms, dating originally from the 17th century but revised in 1959.

# SWAZILAND

*Southern Africa*

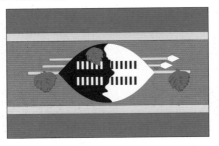

**Kingdom of Swaziland**
**Flag ratio 2:3**
The central emblem of the distinctive flag of Swaziland
depicts the weapons of an Emasotsha warrior: a hide
shield, two assegais, or spears, and a staff. Also featured
are the blue plumes of a widowbird, traditionally
regarded as Swazi royal ornaments. The background
to the emblem is taken from the flag of the Swazi
Pioneer Corps, who served with the British Army in
World War II. Swaziland regained its independence
from Britain in 1968, the new flag having been
adopted the preceding year.

*Scandinavia*

# SWEDEN

**Kingdom of Sweden**
**Flag ratio 5:8**

The present flag was officially adopted in 1906, but
a similar version was first recorded in pictures from
as far back as the 16th century. Its colours were
probably taken from the national coat of arms, of
three gold crowns on a blue field, which originated
in the 14th century. Like Norway, Finland and Iceland,
Sweden fell under Danish influence in the Middle
Ages, and the design of its flag may be based on that
of the Danes, with the off-centre Scandinavian cross
marking it immediately as one of the Norse nations.
Like Iceland, Finland, Norway and Denmark, its naval
ensign is of the distinctive swallowtail or swallowtail-
with-tongue shape.

# SWITZERLAND

*Western Europe*

**Swiss Confederation**
**Flag ratio 1:1**

Although the flag of Switzerland was not officially adopted until 1848, it had actually been in use as the Swiss emblem since the 14th century. It was the banner of Schwyz, one of the original three cantons that founded the Confederation in 1291 for mutual self-defence against the Hapsburgs. At the Battle of Laupern in 1339 it was used to distinguish the soldiers of the Confederation from their opponents. Although the country was occupied by Napoleonic France from 1798 until 1815, its neutrality was ultimately guaranteed under the 1815 Treaty of Paris.

*Middle East*

# SYRIA

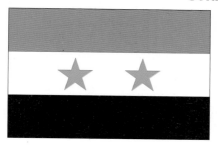

**Syrian Arab Republic**
**Flag ratio 2:3**
Syria has changed its flag five times in its 60 years as
an independent state. The colours of all six flags have
been those of the Pan-Arab movement (black, white,
red and green). These were used initially by many
Arab regions as an anti-Ottoman Empire device.
After the Ottoman Empire collapsed, they became
an expression of Arab solidarity. Each flag change has
reflected contemporary Syrian alliances. The present
flag, in use since 1980, was first used in 1958–61, when
Syria and Egypt formed the United Arab Republic.
At the time the two stars stood for the two member
states.

# TAIWAN

*Eastern Asia*

**Republic of China**

**Flag ratio 2:3**

The island of Taiwan became home to the Chinese
Nationalist forces in 1949, after their defeat by
Communist forces on the Chinese mainland. The flag
they brought had been used as their party flag from
1914, soon after China became a republic. When the
Kuomintang formed the government of China from
1928 until 1949, this became the national flag.

The 12-rayed sun symbolises unceasing progress,
each ray meaning an hour of day and an hour of night.
The colours represent qualities; red for selfless sacrifice,
blue for equality and white for purity. It has also been
said that the flag represents the white sun in a blue
sky over the fertile red land.

*Western Asia* **TAJIKISTAN**

**Republic of Tajikistan**
**Flag ratio 1:2**
Tajikistan was the last of the old republics of the USSR
to adopt a new flag. To date, limited information is
available about the significance of the design, which
features a gold crown and an arc of seven stars
centred in a white band, with bands of red and green
above and below. The colours of red, white and green
are the same as those chosen in 1953 for the flag of
the Tajik Soviet Socialist Republic; this featured a red
flag with a band of white and a smaller band of
green. The new flag was adopted in November 1992.

# TANZANIA

*East Africa*

**United Republic of Tanzania**
**Flag ratio 2:3**

Tanzania was formed in 1964, following the union of the two newly independent states of Tanganyika (1961) and Zanzibar (1963). The flag of the new state combined elements from both the old ones. Tanganyika's flag at independence was a horizontal tribar of green–black–green, with yellow fimbriations to the black stripe. Zanzibar's flag at the time of union was a horizontal tricolour of blue, black and green. The new flag kept the colours of Tanganyika and added Zanzibar's blue, now in a diagonal rather than horizontal pattern. Green is for the land and agriculture, blue is for the sea, black is for the people and yellow for mineral wealth.

*Eastern Asia*

# THAILAND

**Kingdom of Thailand**
**Flag ratio 2:3**
The Trairanga (tricolour), the national flag of Thailand, has been used since 1917. The country was the ancient Kingdom of Siam. Until 1916 the flag was red with a white elephant, the national emblem. A simpler flag, with the colours in five stripes of red and white, was adopted in 1916. In 1917 the centre stripe was changed to blue. The blue stripe is for monarchy, white for Buddhism, the national religion, and red for the life-blood of the people. The country's name was changed from Siam to Thailand in 1939, but the flag was unaltered.

# TOGO

*West Africa*

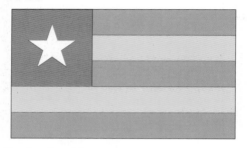

**Togolese Republic**
**Flag ratio 3:5**

Like so many other West African states, the flag of Togo uses the Pan-African colours, first adopted by neighbouring Ghana, as an expression of African unity. In Togo's case, the colours are meant also to be significant in their own right: green representing both hope and agriculture, one of the mainstays of the economy; yellow, for the country's mineral deposits; and red symbolising the independence struggle. The star on the Togo flag is white rather than the black normally used on African flags, and represents national purity. The flag was adopted in 1960, on the country's independence from France.

*Pacific Ocean*

# TONGA

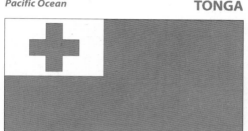

**Kingdom of Tonga**

**Flag ratio 1:2**

The Kingdom of Tonga was established in the mid-19th century, and its flag was designed shortly thereafter. It was officially adopted in 1875 on the understanding that it would never be changed. The red field with its white canton and red couped cross (one whose arms do not extend to the edges of its field) all represent the sacrifice and blood of Christ, and express the islanders' absolute commitment to Wesleyan Methodism. The islands became a British protectorate in 1900 but regained their independence in 1970 and retained their flag.

# TRINIDAD AND TOBAGO    *Caribbean*

**Republic of Trinidad and Tobago**
**Flag ratio 3:5**

The flag of Trinidad and Tobago dates officially from the time of the islands' independence from Britain (1962) and its colours are symbolic. Red represents the vitality of the land and people and the energy and warmth of the sun; black symbolises the people's dedication and unity of purpose, and the wealth of the land; while white stands for the sea which bounds the islands, the purity of national aspirations, and the equality of all. Together, the colours represent the elements of fire, earth and water encompassing the islands. The same colours are used in the shield of the national arms, which were also adopted at the time of independence.

*North Africa*

# TUNISIA

**Republic of Tunisia**
**Flag ratio 2:3**
Tunisia's flag was deliberately designed to look like that of Turkey. The Turks controlled the country from the 16th century, and the flag was adopted in 1835 with the intention of identifying Tunisia as an Ottoman possession. The crescent and star are traditional Ottoman as well as Islamic symbols. The flag survived throughout the French Protectorate (1881–1956) and was retained on independence in 1956. As in the other French North African possessions, the tricolour did not influence the flag officially adopted after independence.

# TURKEY

*Middle East*

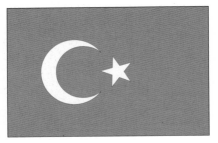

**Republic of Turkey**
**Flag ratio 2:3**
Turkey's white crescent moon and five-pointed star
on a red field is one of the most distinctive of flags.
It evolved finally into its present shape in the last
century. Red was the traditional colour of the
Ottoman Empire, of which Turkey was the heart,
and although the star and crescent have come to
be identified as Islamic symbols, their origins are
obscure, and they may well pre-date both Islam and
Christianity, in which they also have a significance.
Despite its imperial association, the flag was retained
in 1923 by Mustafa Kemal, renamed Atatürk, under
whose leadership the country became a modern,
secular republic.

*Western Asia* # TURKMENISTAN

**Republic of Turkmenistan**
**Flag ratio 2:3**

Turkmenistan's flag was adopted in 1992, shortly after the break-up of the USSR, of which the country had been part. Its green field and crescent moon identify the country as a Muslim state. The vertical band at the hoist is a depiction of a Turkestani carpet. The five carpet patterns are for the five main tribes comprising the state. These five elements are repeated in the stars set near the crescent. In 1997 the wreath from the UN flag was added, to signify the country's wish for peace and international cooperation. The carpet patterns were modified slightly in 2001.

# TURKS AND CAICOS ISLANDS

*Caribbean*

**Colony of the Turks and Caicos Islands**
**Flag ratio 1:2**

The Turks Islands were discovered in the 16th century and colonised in the 17th by Bermudian settlers. The Caicos Islands were ruled jointly with the Turks from 1848. From the 19th century all the islands were administered by Jamaica, despite local protests, and they did not become separate until Jamaican independence in 1962. The islands have been a British dependent territory (see corner flag) since 1976, and they fly the Blue Ensign with the badge from the island arms in the fly. A conch shell, a spiny lobster (langoustines are a major export) and a turk's head cactus, all local flora and fauna, feature. This flag was approved in 1968 but an earlier flag had a different badge.

*Pacific Ocean*

# TUVALU

**Tuvalu**
**Flag ratio 1:2**

Tuvalu and Kiribati were united as the Gilbert and Ellice Islands until 1975, when the Ellice Islands left, becoming independent as Tuvalu in 1978. A pale Blue Ensign was adopted (reflecting its links with Britain) with nine gold stars in the fly to show the islands' geographical position. In 1995 a new government changed the flag to drop the British connection: three unequal horizontal bands of red, blue and red were separated by white fimbriations. The stars changed to white, reduced to eight (one island is uninhabited) and the arms appeared in a white triangle at the hoist in the blue band. When the regime fell in 1997 the original flag was restored, with the stars at different angles.

# UGANDA

*East Africa*

**Republic of Uganda**
**Flag ratio 2:3**
The flag of Uganda was adopted on independence
from Britain in 1962 and, despite four coups since
then, has remained the same to the present day.
It comprises six equal horizontal bands of black,
yellow and red, and the colours are symbolic: black
represents the people; yellow stands for the sun,
which shines directly overhead in this equatorial
country; and red represents the brotherhood of all
peoples. The central white disc is charged with a
crested crane.

*Eastern Europe* # UKRAINE

**Ukraine**

**Flag ratio 2:3**

Ukraine's blue and yellow bicolour is rooted in its history. The colours featured on the coat of arms of a medieval Ukrainian principality, and on banners in the 13th-century fight to expel invading Mongol forces. They resurfaced in 1848, when Ukraine was one of the few Slavic areas not to adopt the Russian colours. As well as historical interpretations, the flag's colours have a modern meaning: blue is for the sky and yellow the golden wheat of the Steppes. Ukraine became independent of empire in 1918 and a version of the bicolour was adopted, only to be set aside when the country became part of the USSR. In 1992, the parliament was able to adopt the flag again.

# UNITED ARAB EMIRATES *Middle East*

**United Arab Emirates**
**Flag ratio 1:2**
Red was traditionally associated with the Kharijite peoples of Southeast Arabia, while white was used on most state flags in this part of the Gulf in the wake of an 1820 maritime treaty with Britain. Consequently, red and white were the colours of the flags in six of the seven sheikdoms which came to form the United Arab Emirates in 1971. All seven members (Abu Dhabi, Dubai, Sharjah, Rasal Khaimah, Fujeirah, Ajman and Umm al Qaiwan) retain their own flags and arms, but the UAE has adopted the Pan-Arab movement colours – red, green, white and black – expressive of Arab nationalism and unity, as well as having the red and white colours of the individual states.

*Western Europe* **UNITED KINGDOM**

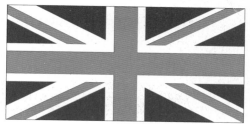

**United Kingdom of Great Britain and Northern Ireland**
**Flag ratio 1:2**

The Union Flag, or Union Jack as it is often called, combines the flags of Scotland, England and Ireland. It its first form it appeared after King James VI of Scotland became King of England in 1603. In 1606 a flag was designed, combining the St Andrew flag of Scotland (a white saltire on blue) and the St George flag of England (a red cross on white). A white fimbriation separated the red and blue. This was later reserved for use at sea by the Royal Navy. In 1801 a red saltire was added, counterchanged with the Scottish saltire, when Ireland joined the United Kingdom. This is now the unofficial but accepted national flag on land.

# UNITED STATES OF AMERICA

*North America*

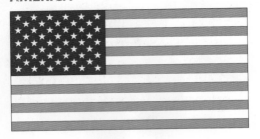

**United States of America**

**Flag ratio 10:19**

The first US flag in 1776 had 13 red and white stripes for the 13 colonies, and the British Union flag in the canton. After independence was declared, the Union Flag no longer fitted. On 14 June 1777, the American Congress adopted a new flag, keeping the stripes but adding a canton of 13 white stars on blue. When more states were added, it was decided, in 1818, that 13 stripes remain, but that a star be added each time a new state entered the Union. There have been 28 versions of the flag, the present one dating from 1960, after Hawaii became a state. The US flag has been influential in the designs of others (see Malaysia, Liberia and Togo), and was the first to use stars.

*South America*

# URUGUAY

**Eastern Republic of Uruguay**

**Flag ratio 2:3**

Uruguay's 19th-century history was dominated by a struggle for independence against both Brazil and Argentina, after winning freedom from Spain. The present flag was adopted in 1830. The nine white and blue stripes are for the nine original provinces. The sun is a version of the Sun of May from the Argentinian flag, because the Argentinian declaration of independence applied also to Uruguay at the time. Uruguay's first flag was a blue–white–blue Argentinian tribar, with a red diagonal stripe. This was the flag used by José Artigas, the national hero who first fought to end Spanish rule. That flag now forms the jack of the Uruguayan Navy, and is the flag of Artigas' home province.

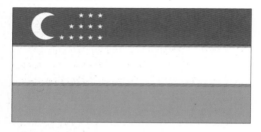

# UZBEKISTAN

*Western Asia*

**Republic of Uzbekistan**
**Flag ratio 1:2**
The new flag of the republic, formerly a part of the USSR, was adopted in 1991. Its colours are symbolic: the blue stands for Uzbekistan's waters and skies, the white for peace, and the green for fertility and nature. The crescent and stars are traditional Muslim symbols, and the 12 stars here are symbolic of the months of the Islamic calendar. The blue colour also recalls the colour of Timur, a former khan, under whose rule in the 14th century the whole region enjoyed a golden age of expansion and prosperity.

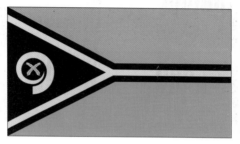

*Pacific Ocean*

# VANUATU

**Republic of Vanuatu**
**Flag ratio 3:5**

This Pacific archipelago was ruled jointly by France and Britain as the New Hebrides until 1980. At independence the name was changed to Vanuatu. The flag adopted was in the colours of the Vanuaaku Party, the leading political party of the time. The yellow 'Y' refers to the geographical distribution of the islands. In the black triangle are a boar's tusk and two crossed namele fern leaves, representing the traditional way of life of the islanders. Red is for the blood shed for freedom, green represents the fertility of the islands, black is for the people and yellow for prosperity.

# VATICAN CITY

*Western Europe*

**State of the Vatican City**
**Flag ratio 1:1**
The Vatican flag colours derive from the emblem in
the fly. They were adopted as the papal colours by
Pius VII in 1808, and the flag was used from 1825 until
the unification of Italy in 1870, when all provinces,
including the Papal States, were joined. In the 1929
Lateran Treaty, Italy granted the Papal States the right
to a separate existence, confined to the Vatican City.
The emblem itself shows the three-tiered papal
crown, signifying the three types of temporal power
– legislative, executive and judicial – vested in the
pope, while the crossed keys below symbolise his
spiritual authority from the bestowing of the keys
of Heaven by Christ on St Peter, the first pope.

*South America*

# VENEZUELA

**Bolivarian Republic of Venezuela**
**Flag ratio 2:3**
Venezuela, Colombia and Ecuador have similar flags,
based on that of South America's 19th-century
liberators Francisco de Miranda and Simón Bolívar.
The countries joined in federation, as Gran Colombia,
from 1819 until 1830, but the proportions of the bands
on Venezuela's flag were later made equal to distinguish
it. The colours stood for the golden land of South
America (yellow) separated by sea (blue) from imperial
Spain (red). The seven stars represented the original
provinces. The state flag has the arms in the canton:
in a shield is depicted the independent land, with two
cornucopias above. A scroll below recalls the dates of
independence and the adoption of a federal constitution.

# VIETNAM

*Eastern Asia*

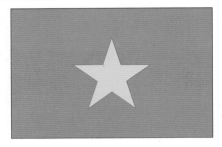

**Socialist Republic of Vietnam**
**Flag ratio 2:3**

Vietnam, as part of French Indochina, was occupied by the Japanese during World War II, and the ultimately victorious national resistance movement, led by Ho Chi Minh, adopted the flag they had used during the war as the national flag in 1945. This was basically the same as the flag in use today, itself obviously influenced by the old Soviet flag, with the star of Communism in the centre. The country was partitioned into north and south after the French left in 1954, and the government in the north began a long war to overcome the southern government and their American allies, and reunite the country, their aims finally being achieved in 1976.

*Caribbean*

# VIRGIN ISLANDS (US)

**Virgin Islands**
**Flag ratio 2:3**

The Virgin Islands of the US are an American dependency (see corner flag and also British Virgin Islands). They were bought from Denmark in 1917, and this territorial flag has been used since 1921. In the centre of the white field is an emblem based on the US coat of arms, consisting of an American eagle with wings outstretched and on its breast a shield containing 13 vertical stripes in red and white beneath a blue chief (the top part of the shield). In its claws are an olive branch to symbolise peace, and three arrows, representing defence. The emblem appears between the initial letters of the islands' name, 'V' and 'I' in blue.

# WALES

*Western Europe*

Wales
**Flag ratio 3:5**
Wales was the only country to enter the third
millennium with the same emblem it had used at the
beginning of the second, the Red Dragon. The legend
of the Red Dragon dates back to early medieval
times, when a Welsh prince dreamed that the
Red Dragon of Wales defeated the White Dragon of
the Saxons. Today it appears on the white and green
livery colours of the Tudor dynasty, which ruled
England from 1485 until 1603. This flag was adopted
by the Welsh Assembly as the official flag of Wales.
Like the flags of St Andrew and St George, this flag is
used only on land.

*Pacific Ocean*

# WALLIS AND FUTUNA

**Territory of the Wallis and Futuna Islands**
**Flag ratio 2:3**
The use of the tricolour in the canton of this flag
indicates that the islands are a French possession
(see corner flag). As in the flags of many other Pacific
states, the red and white colours were traditionally
used by the people of the islands. The unusual motif
set in the fly which looks at first glance like a cross or
saltire is actually four triangles, representing the four
main islands of the group.

# YEMEN

*Middle East*

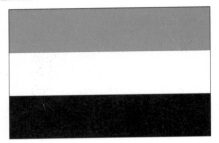

**Republic of Yemen**

**Flag ratio 2:3**

The former Yemen Arab Republic (North Yemen) and the People's Democratic Republic of Yemen (South Yemen) united in 1990, and the new country's flag is an amalgamation of the two states' flags. The red, white and black tricolour shows support for the Pan-Arab ideals of Arab nationalism and unity. The green star from the flag of the Yemen Arab Republic, and the blue triangle and red star from the flag of the People's Democratic Republic of Yemen, have both been dropped. The flag's pattern suggests a compromise between the officially secular former People's Democratic Republic of Yemen and the more officially Islamic-orientated Yemen Arab Republic to the north.

*Southern Africa*  **ZAMBIA**

**Republic of Zambia**
**Flag ratio 2:3**
This national flag is unusual in that its devices are set
in the fly rather than in the hoist. The colours are mainly
those of the once-dominant United Nationalist
Independence Party, or UNIP, in 1964 when Zambia,
then Northern Rhodesia, won its independence.
The interpretation now put on the colours is that the
green field stands for agriculture, and the red, black
and orange bars signify respectively the struggle for
freedom, the people, and copper, the main national
mineral resource. The eagle first appeared on the old
colonial coat of arms but has now been adapted for
the modern arms and for the flag, and symbolises
the national spirit, hopes for the future and freedom.

# ZIMBABWE

*Southern Africa*

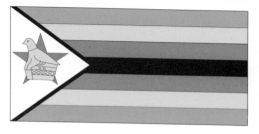

**Republic of Zimbabwe**
**Flag ratio 1:2**
The stripes of the Zimbabwean flag echo the colours
of the Zimbabwe African National Union which led
the state at its founding in 1980. The colours are
symbolic: green for agriculture; yellow mineral wealth;
red the freedom struggle; and at the centre, black for
the people. Red, yellow and green, often with black
motifs, are also the colours of the Pan-African
movement of African unity. The black-fimbriated white
triangle on the hoist symbolises peace and the red
star the government's socialist ideals. The bird is
traditional, first found carved on soapstone in the
ancient ruined city of Zimbabwe; long the national
emblem, it represents a link with the country's heritage.

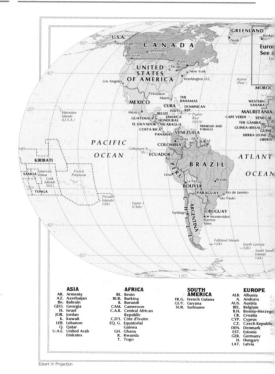

**ASIA**
- AR. Armenia
- AZ. Azerbaijan
- Bn. Bahrain
- GEO. Georgia
- IS. Israel
- JOR. Jordan
- K. Kuwait
- LEB. Lebanon
- Q. Qatar
- U.A.E. United Arab Emirates

**AFRICA**
- BE. Benin
- BUR. Burkina
- B. Burundi
- CAM. Cameroon
- C.A.R. Central African Republic
- C.D'I. Côte d'Ivoire
- EQ. G. Equatorial Guinea
- GH. Ghana
- R. Rwanda
- T. Togo

**SOUTH AMERICA**
- FR.G. French Guiana
- GUY. Guyana
- SUR. Suriname

**EUROPE**
- ALB. Albania
- A. Andorra
- AUS. Austria
- BEL. Belgium
- B.H. Bosnia-Herzegov
- CR. Croatia
- CYP. Cyprus
- CZ. Czech Republic
- DEN. Denmark
- EST. Estonia
- GER. Germany
- H. Hungary
- LAT. Latvia

RUSSIAN FEDERATION
Arctic Circle
Moscow  Yekaterinburg  Novosibirsk  Magadan
bottom of page
KAZAKHSTAN  Astana
MONGOLIA  Ulaanbaatar
TURKMEN-  KYRGYZSTAN  Beijing  N. KOREA  JAPAN
IRAN  ISTAN  TAJIKISTAN  CHINA  S. KOREA  Tōkyō
Tehrān  AFGHAN-  Islamabad  Shanghai
LIBYA  EGYPT  SAUDI  ISTAN  NEPAL  BHUTAN  TAIWAN
Tripoli  Cairo  Riyadh  ARABIA  BANGLA-  Ha Nôi
GER  ARABIA  PAKISTAN  DESH  MYANMAR
Khartoum  ERITREA  YEMEN  INDIA  THAILAND  Manila  PHILIPPINES
CHAD  SUDAN  DJIBOUTI  CAMBODIA
ERIA  C.A.R.  ETHIOPIA  SRI  BRUNEI
CAM  UGANDA  KENYA  LANKA  MALAYSIA  PALAU
DEM.  SEYCHELLES  SINGAPORE  INDONESIA
REP.  TANZANIA  Jakarta
CONGO
NGOLA  ZAMBIA  MOZAMBIQUE  INDIAN  EAST
ZIMBABWE  MADAGASCAR  MAURITIUS  OCEAN  TIMOR
MIBIA  BOTS-  Réunion  AUSTRALIA
WANA  SWAZILAND  (Fr.)
REP. OF  LESOTHO
SOUTH  Perth
AFRICA
Town

PACIFIC
OCEAN
Tropic of Cancer
Northern
Mariana
Islands  MARSHALL
(U.S.A.)  ISLANDS
Equator
FEDERATED STATES
OF MICRONESIA
NAURU  KIRIBATI
PAPUA  SOLOMON  TUVALU
NEW  ISLANDS
GUINEA  VANUATU  FIJI
Port
Moresby  New  2002
Caledonia
(Fr.)  Tropic of Capricorn

Sydney
Canberra
NEW
ZEALAND
Wellington

Kerguelen
(Fr.)

SOUTHERN OCEAN

NTARCTICA

H.  Lithuania
X.  Luxembourg
M.  Macedonia
O.  Moldova
H.  Netherlands
F.  Russian Federation
E.  Serbia and Montenegro
L.  Slovakia
S.  Slovenia
V.  Switzerland

ICELAND
Reykjavík  NORWAY  SWEDEN  FINLAND  RUSSIAN
UNITED  EST.  FEDERATION
KINGDOM  DEN.  LITH.  LAT.  Moscow
REP. OF  NETH.  POLAND  BELARUS
IRELAND  London  BEL.  CZ.  UKRAINE
LUX.  REP.  SVK.  GEO.
FRANCE  AUS.  HUN.  ROMANIA
Paris  SW.  BIH.  BULGARIA  TURKEY  AR.  AZ.
ITALY  ALB.  GREECE  Tehrān
SPAIN  Algiers  TUNISIA  CYP.  SYRIA
PORTUGAL

Europe 1:170M

© Collins Bartholomew Ltd

# LIST OF FLAGS

Afghanistan
Åland Islands
Albania
Algeria
American Samoa
Andorra
Angola
Anguilla
Antigua and
  Barbuda
Argentina
Armenia
Aruba
Australia
Austria
Azerbaijan
Bahamas
Bahrain
Bangladesh
Barbados
Belarus
Belgium
Belize
Benin
Bermuda
Bhutan

Bolivia
Bosnia and
  Herzegovina
Botswana
Brazil
British Indian
  Ocean Territory
British Virgin
  Islands
Brunei
Bulgaria
Burkina Faso
Burundi
Cambodia
Cameroon
Canada
Cape Verde
Cayman Islands
Central African
  Republic
Chad
Chile
China
Colombia
Comoros
Congo

Cook Islands
Costa Rica
Côte d'Ivoire
Croatia
Cuba
Cyprus
Czech Republic
Democratic
  Republic of
  Congo
Denmark
Djibouti
Dominica
Dominican
  Republic
East Timor
Ecuador
Egypt
El Salvador
England
Equatorial Guinea
Eritrea
Estonia
Ethiopia
Falkland Islands
Faroe Islands

Fiji
Finland
France
French Polynesia
Friesian Islands
Gabon
Gambia
Georgia
Germany
Ghana
Gibraltar
Greece
Greenland
Grenada
Guam
Guatemala
Guernsey
Guinea
Guinea-Bissau
Guyana
Haiti
Honduras
Hong Kong
Hungary
Iceland
India
Indonesia

Iran
Iraq
Ireland
Isle of Man
Israel
Italy
Jamaica
Japan
Jersey
Jordan
Kazakhstan
Kenya
Kiribati
Kuwait
Kyrgyzstan
Laos
Latvia
Lebanon
Lesotho
Liberia
Libya
Liechtenstein
Lithuania
Luxembourg
Macedonia
Madagascar
Malawi

Malaysia
Maldives
Mali
Malta
Marshall Islands
Mauritania
Mauritius
Mexico
Micronesia
Moldova
Monaco
Mongolia
Montserrat
Morocco
Mozambique
Myanmar
Namibia
Nauru
Nepal
Netherlands
Netherlands
  Antilles
New Zealand
Nicaragua
Niger
Nigeria
Niue

North Korea
Northern Marianas
Norway
Oman
Pakistan
Palau
Palestine
Panama
Papua New Guinea
Paraguay
Peru
Philippines
Pitcairn Islands
Poland
Portugal
Puerto Rico
Qatar
Romania
Russia
Rwanda
St Helena
St Kitts and Nevis
St Lucia
St Vincent and the Grenadines
Samao
San Marino

São Tomé and Principe
Saudi Arabia
Scotland
Senegal
Serbia and Montenegro
Seychelles
Sierra Leone
Singapore
Slovakia
Slovenia
Solomon Islands
Somalia
South Africa
South Korea
Spain
Sri Lanka
Sudan
Suriname
Swaziland
Sweden
Switzerland
Syria
Taiwan
Tajikistan
Tanzania
Thailand

Togo
Tonga
Trinidad and Tobago
Tunisia
Turkey
Turkmenistan
Turks and Caicos Islands
Tuvalu
Uganda
Ukraine
United Arab Emirates
United Kingdom
United States of America
Uruguay
Uzbekistan
Vanuatu
Vatican City
Venezuela
Vietnam
Virgin Islands (US)
Wales
Wallis and Futuna
Yemen
Zambia
Zimbabwe